Academic Writing and Referencing for your

Education

Degree

CRITICAL
STUDY SKILLS

Critical Study Skills for Education Students

Our new series of study skills texts for education and initial teacher training students has four key titles to help you succeed in your degree:

Studying for your Education Degree

Academic Writing and Referencing for your Education Degree

Critical Thinking Skills for your Education Degree

Communication Skills for your Education Degree

Register with **Critical Publishing** to:

- be the first to know about forthcoming education titles;
- find out more about our new series;
- sign up for our regular newsletter for special offers, discount codes and more.

Visit our website at: **www.criticalpublishing.com**

Our titles are also available in a range of electronic formats. To order please go to our website www.criticalpublishing.com or contact our distributor NBN International by telephoning 01752 202301 or emailing orders@nbninternational.com.

Academic Writing and Referencing for your Education Degree

Education Degree

CRITICAL STUDY SKILLS

JANE BOTTOMLEY, STEVEN PRYJMACHUK AND DAVID WAUGH

First published in 2018 by Critical Publishing Ltd

British Library Cataloguing in Publication Data
A CIP record for this book is available from the British Library

ISBN: 978-1-912096-78-7

This book is also available in the following e-book formats:

MOBI: 978-1-912096-77-0
EPUB: 978-1-912096-76-3
Adobe e-book reader: 978-1-912096-75-6

Text and cover design by Out of House Limited
Project management by Out of House Publishing
Printed and bound in Great Britain by 4edge, Essex

Critical Publishing
3 Connaught Road
St Albans
AL3 5RX

www.criticalpublishing.com

Paper from responsible sources

Contents

Acknowledgements

We would like to thank the many university and education students who have inspired us to write these books. Special thanks are due to Anita Gill. Our appreciation also goes to Andrew Drummond and Maureen Finn for their comments on specific parts of the manuscript.

Jane Bottomley, Steven Pryjmachuk and David Waugh

Meet the series editor and authors

Jane Bottomley

is the **Series Editor** for *Critical Study Skills* and a co-author of all books in the series. She is a Senior Language Tutor at the University of Manchester and a Senior Fellow of the British Association of Lecturers in English for Academic Purposes (BALEAP). She has helped students from a wide range of disciplines to improve their academic skills and achieve their study goals. She has previously published on scientific writing.

Steven Pryjmachuk

is Professor of Mental Health Nursing Education in the School of Health Science's Division of Nursing, Midwifery and Social Work at the University of Manchester and a Senior Fellow of the Higher Education Academy. His teaching, clinical and research work has centred largely on supporting and facilitating individuals – be they students, patients or colleagues – to develop, learn or care independently.

David Waugh

is Associate Professor of Education at Durham University where he is subject leader for Primary English. He has written more than 40 books on education and has taught in four schools, as well as teaching undergraduates and postgraduates. He has worked in education in universities for 28 years and also regularly teaches in schools, using the four children's novels he has written as a stimulus for reading, writing and discussion.

Introduction

Academic Writing and Referencing is the second book in the *Critical Study Skills for Education* series. The *Critical Study Skills for Education* series supports student teachers and other education professionals as they embark on their undergraduate degree programmes. It is aimed at all student teachers, including those who have come to university straight from A levels, and those who have travelled a different route, perhaps returning to education after working or raising a family. The books will be of use both to students from the UK, and international students who are preparing to study in a new culture – and perhaps in a second language. The books also include guidance for students with specific learning difficulties.

Academic Writing and Referencing provides you with the knowledge, language, skills and strategies that you need in order to develop your academic writing skills and succeed in writing assignments. It introduces you to typical education writing assignments, and explores important areas such as the writing process, coherence, referring to sources, academic style and grammatical accuracy. It helps you to develop important skills such as planning and editing. It reflects the centrality of criticality in writing by referring to it throughout the different chapters, and shows how it is achieved through a multi-layered approach, including development of stance and argument, choice of language, and considered reference to sources. The book also helps you to prepare your work to a professional standard for submission.

Between them, the authors have many years' experience of both teaching practice and education, and academic study skills. All the information, text extracts and activities in the book have a clear education focus and are often directly linked to the **Teachers' Standards**. There is also reference to relevant institutional bodies, books and journals throughout.

The many activities in the book include reflections, case studies, top tips, checklists and tasks. There are also advanced skills sections, which highlight particular knowledge and skills that you will need towards the end of your degree programme – or perhaps if you go on to postgraduate study. The activities often require you to work things out and discover things for yourself, a learning technique which is commonly used in universities. For many activities, there is no right or wrong answer – they might simply require you to reflect on your experience or situations you are likely to encounter at university; for tasks which require a particular response, there is an answer key at the back of the book.

These special features throughout the book are clearly signalled by icons to help you recognise them:

 Learning outcomes;

 Quick quiz or example exam questions/assessment tasks;

 Reflection (a reflective task or activity);

 Task;

 Case studies;

Top tips;

 Checklist;

 Advanced skills information;

 Answer provided at the back of the book.

Students with limited experience of academic life in the UK will find it helpful to work through the book systematically; more experienced students may wish to 'dip in and out' of the book. Whichever approach you adopt, handy **cross references** signalled in the margins will help you quickly find the information that you need to focus on or revisit.

There are four appendices at the back of the book which you can consult as you work through the text.

We hope that this book will help you to develop as an academic writer and to become a confident member of your academic writing community. We hope it will help you to achieve your goals and produce written work to the very best of your abilities.

A note on terminology

In the context of this book, the term 'education' should be taken to include 'educational studies and teacher education', wherever this is not explicitly stated.

Chapter 1
Academic writing:
text, process and criticality

Learning outcomes

After reading this chapter you will:

- understand what it means to be part of the academic writing community;

- be aware of the different text types you might need to produce as a student teacher;

- have developed an effective, systematic approach to the academic writing process;

- understand what it means to write critically;

- have learned about the foundations of different academic text types in education, in particular, the critical essay.

There are many challenges facing you as you embark on your education degree. You need to assimilate a great deal of information, and engage in new ideas and intellectual processes. What's more, you need to become proficient in academic writing, and learn how to produce the different types of text that are common in education.

Academic writing is central to your university studies, as written assignments and exams will be one of the main ways in which you are assessed. This chapter explores the nature of academic writing in universities, and helps you to develop an effective, systematic approach to the academic writing process. All assignments are different, and universities vary slightly in terms of the types of writing assignments they employ. This chapter focuses on some general principles which can be applied to most academic writing, including what it means to write 'critically'. It also discusses some of the most common features of individual text types in your discipline, with a particular focus on the critical essay.

Academic writing at university: a new start?

Reflection

1) Do you enjoy writing? Why/Why not?
2) What kind of things have you written in the past (eg essays, reports, exams, articles, blogs, stories, poems)?

1

3) Do you have recent experience of writing academic essays? (If English is not your first language, were these in English or your first language?)

4) What comments have teachers or other people made about your writing in the past?

5) How do you feel about starting your first/next written assignment at university?

Education students in the UK come from a range of backgrounds: some come straight from A levels (or Scottish Highers); some have been away from formal education for some time, maybe working and/or bringing up a family; some come from other countries to study in the UK. This means that students starting university differ in terms of their writing abilities, their experience of academic writing, and how confident they feel about tackling written assessments.

So where do you fit in?

You may be feeling confident. You may be relishing the prospect of writing your first assignment, seeing it as an exciting opportunity to explore your subject and demonstrate your knowledge and ideas. You may be able to draw on recent experience of academic writing and positive feedback from teachers.

Conversely, you may be feeling rather apprehensive about your first written assignment. Like many students, you perhaps see academic writing as one of the most difficult challenges of university life. There are a number of reasons why you may be feeling apprehensive. You might not have much experience of academic writing. Or maybe you do have experience, but it might have been a long time ago, or in your mother tongue, not English. You may have struggled with writing in the past and received some negative comments from teachers. All of these things can make the prospect of that first written assignment rather daunting.

CROSS
REFERENCE

Chapter 2,
Coherent
texts and
arguments,
Editing and
redrafting for
coherence,
The truth
about writing!

When starting to write at university, it is important for students to draw on any strengths they have in terms of ability and experience. But it is also important for all students to identify aspects of their writing which can be improved on. At university, you are part of a **writing community**, comprised of students, lecturers and researchers, and all members of that community are constantly striving to improve as writers, even those who publish in journals and books.

You should commit yourself to improving as a writer throughout your degree programme, and beyond, in your professional life. It is not a question of achieving perfection; it is rather a case of committing yourself to making many small improvements over time, and not giving up when faced with a disappointment or hurdle. University lecturers see many students develop into very good writers after a shaky start. What these students have in common is a positive attitude, an ability to reflect on and critically assess their own work, and a willingness to seek and act on advice.

This book will support you in your development as a writer by helping you to approach writing in a systematic way. It will enable you to:

- analyse and respond to writing tasks;
- plan and structure your writing effectively;
- achieve clarity and coherence in your writing;
- produce writing which is accurate and academic in style;
- write critically in assignments;
- use and reference sources appropriately;
- prepare assignments to a high professional standard for submission.

This chapter sets you on your way by exploring the context of academic writing at university and providing guidance on how to approach writing assignments during your education degree.

Academic writing for education undergraduates

Undergraduate education students may be asked to produce a number of different types of academic writing, including essays, written reflections, exams, reports, reviews of journal articles, and dissertations. This chapter sets out a general approach to academic writing that will help you with all types of assignments. It also provides specific information on essays, written reflections, exams and dissertations. Advice on practical writing tasks in education is provided in *Communication Skills for your Education Degree*.

- **Essays**. There are different types of essays. The main one, sometimes called a 'critical' or 'analytical' essay, requires you to explore a particular topic in depth, usually in response to a question or statement, and to explain your own viewpoint, or 'stance', supported by arguments and evidence. A 'reflective' essay requires you to analyse and evaluate a particular experience, explaining its impact on your understanding and future practice.
- **Written reflections**. Student teachers are often required to produce written reflections on their teaching, usually as part of a **professional portfolio**.
- **Exams**. In exams, you may be required to provide short or long written responses to questions or statements. These are usually designed to demonstrate that you have assimilated and understood the core work covered in a particular module. They may require you to recall factual information and/or to explain and support your viewpoint on a particular issue you have examined as part of your studies.
- **Dissertations**. A dissertation is a long evidence-based or research-focused essay written in the final year of your undergraduate studies.

Each of these types of academic writing will be discussed in more detail later in the chapter.

CROSS
REFERENCE

Communication Skills for your Education Degree

CROSS
REFERENCE

Studying for your Education Degree, Chapter 6, Assessment

The writing process

Writing is a process and it involves a number of stages, including:

- 'unpacking' (analysing and understanding) the writing task and any guidelines provided;
- drawing up a provisional plan/outline;
- identifying relevant material that you need to read;
- reading and gathering information;
- drafting, redrafting, editing;
- revisiting and reworking your plan/outline;
- formatting your text;
- double-checking the assessment guidelines;
- proofreading.

It is important to fully engage with the writing process, and to understand that the *writing* process is part of the *learning* process. Writing is not just a question of getting fully formed thoughts down on paper (apart from in exams); it is a way of *clarifying your thinking* on a particular topic. Woodford (1967) put this nicely many years ago:

> The power of writing as an aid in thinking is not often appreciated. Everyone knows that someone who writes successfully gets his thoughts completely in order before he publishes. But it is seldom pointed out that the very act of writing can help to clarify thinking. Put down woolly thoughts on paper, and their wooliness is immediately exposed.

(p 744)

CROSS
REFERENCE

Chapter 2,
Coherent
texts and
arguments,
Editing and
redrafting for
coherence

Top tips

Engaging with the writing process

1) Try to develop good writing habits. Write little and often, especially if you have been away from formal education for a while.

2) Adopt a write-read-edit-read approach to writing (discussed in Chapter 2). When you stop to read what you have written, stand back from the text. Put yourself in the reader's shoes and make sure that everything hangs together, makes sense, and flows smoothly.

3) Try to get some feedback during the writing process. You may have the opportunity to submit a first draft to a lecturer, or you could ask a fellow student to read something and give feedback. If you do ask a friend or fellow student, it's a good idea to ask them to *summarise* what they think you are trying to say. If you only ask them if they understand what you have written, they may just say yes to be polite!

Your exact approach to the writing process will depend on the particular context of the assignment and your individual way of working, but some essential aspects of the writing process are discussed in the following sections.

Approaching a writing assignment

A writer needs an audience, a purpose, and a strategy, and these things are interconnected (Swales and Feak, 2012, p 10). When approaching a writing assignment, ask yourself:

- Who is reading my work? (your audience)
- Why am I writing? (your purpose)
- How will I achieve my purpose? (your strategy)

Your purpose is to meet the requirements of the assignment, and satisfy the needs and expectations of a particular reader. To determine your purpose, you need to analyse the wording of the task or question carefully. It may specify certain aspects of the topic that you should cover, and the verbs it uses, such as 'describe', 'explain', or 'evaluate', will determine how you treat this content. However, notwithstanding these specifications, there is no single 'right answer': different students will respond to a task in different ways. The task, together with your individual approach and strategy, will determine:

- the selection of content (information, arguments, evidence etc);
- the way this content is structured and organised.

The person reading your essay must be able to discern *why* you have included particular content and organised your essay in the way that you have.

The question of the 'reader' is a tricky one. Of course, the actual human being reading your assignment is your university lecturer – probably the one who set the task and taught the module. However, lecturers often ask (or expect) you to imagine a 'hypothetical' or 'target' reader. This is usually someone with a similar level of knowledge to your own, or someone with a similar level of education but who is not an expert in education. Lecturers want you to write for such a reader because they want you to *demonstrate* your understanding, and it can be hard to do this if you assume too much knowledge on the part of the reader. It is not uncommon to ask a student about something which is unclear in their essay, only to have them explain that 'the lecturer already knows this'! But this is not the point. The lecturer wants to know that *you* know this, and that you can explain it to other people, including non-experts, in a clear way. Always ask yourself:

- What can the target reader be expected to know?
- What does the target reader need me to explain?

A good writer anticipates the reader's questions, and does not ask them to guess, fill in gaps, or work out how one thing relates to another.

Analysing a writing assignment

One of the most common – and perhaps surprising – reasons for low marks in written assessments is a failure on the part of the student to read the assignment title or question thoroughly enough. A student may go on to produce something which is interesting and of a good standard, but if they do not directly address the specific task, they will not meet the actual requirements of the assignment and

CROSS REFERENCE

Analysing a writing assignment

CROSS REFERENCE

Appendix 3, Key phrases in assignments

CROSS REFERENCE

Chapter 2, Coherent texts and arguments, Editing and redrafting for coherence; Developing a coherent argument and expressing criticality

CROSS REFERENCE

Appendix 3, Key phrases in assignments

so will end up failing. It is therefore essential to start any assignment by carefully analysing the assignment title or question.

You should read the title or question several times to 'unpack' it and get absolutely clear in your mind what is expected of you. It is helpful to highlight **key terms**, including verbs commonly occurring in academic assignments such as 'assess', 'discuss', and 'compare and contrast'.

Assignments usually come with a set of assessment **guidelines** and marking **descriptors** detailing the various criteria that you need to meet in order to achieve success. These criteria relate to areas such as:

- task achievement;
- content and organisation;
- relevance to teaching practice;
- writing style;
- referencing.

Be sure to read and digest these guidelines and descriptors as they are the very same ones that assessors will use to mark your work.

CROSS
REFERENCE

Studying for your Education Degree, Chapter 6, Assessment, Feedback on academic work

Task

Unpacking essay titles and questions

Look at the essay titles below. What are the key terms? What are you expected to do in your essay? What will be your purpose in writing? What type of content and organisation could help you to achieve this purpose? (Make some notes before you look at the model analyses provided.)

A

Given the many factors which might influence children's engagement with reading, consider the question: 'Can teachers play a significant role in developing positive attitudes to reading in their pupils?'

B

The core skill for teachers is the ability to communicate. Using appropriate evidence, explore the arguments for and against this proposition.

Discussion: unpacking essay titles and questions

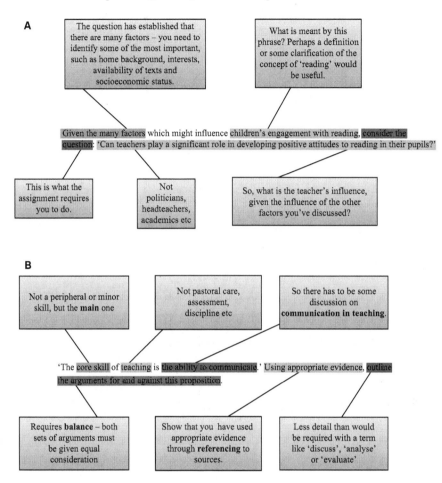

A

The question has established that there are many factors – you need to identify some of the most important, such as home background, interests, availability of texts and socioeconomic status.

What is meant by this phrase? Perhaps a definition or some clarification of the concept of 'reading' would be useful.

Given the many factors which might influence children's engagement with reading, consider the question: 'Can teachers play a significant role in developing positive attitudes to reading in their pupils?'

This is what the assignment requires you to do.

Not politicians, headteachers, academics etc

So, what is the teacher's influence, given the influence of the other factors you've discussed?

B

Not a peripheral or minor skill, but the **main** one

Not pastoral care, assessment, discipline etc

So there has to be some discussion on **communication in teaching**.

'The core skill of teaching is the ability to communicate.' Using appropriate evidence, outline the arguments for and against this proposition.

Requires **balance** – both sets of arguments must be given equal consideration

Show that you have used appropriate evidence through **referencing** to sources.

Less detail than would be required with a term like 'discuss', 'analyse' or 'evaluate'

Planning

Always begin an assignment by considering the constraints of the task: how long it should be and how long you have to write it. You could then draw up a provisional schedule which allocates time to the various sub-tasks. This schedule should leave sufficient time for you to read through and proofread the whole text several times before submitting.

A good piece of writing starts with a good plan or 'outline'. This should be primarily based on your analysis, or 'unpacking', of the task, but it should evolve as you engage in the reading and writing process. Your outline is therefore much more than a list of items related to the assignment topic: it is a developing conceptual representation of your response to the task. For example, in relation to the essay titles analysed above, your outline would reflect your position, or 'stance', in relation to the given topic, ie:

- A: the extent to which you believe, supported by your investigations, that teachers can play a significant role in developing positive attitudes to reading in their pupils

CROSS REFERENCE

Chapter 5, Preparing your work for submission, Editing and proofreading your final text

CROSS REFERENCE

Writing critically

- B: your assessment of the evidence you find to support or challenge the main proposition that communication is a core skill of teaching

CROSS
REFERENCE

Chapter 2,
Coherent
texts and
arguments,
Planning for
coherence

An outline should identify key sections of the text (with possible headings and subheadings), and, in a critical essay, the arguments and evidence that would feature in each one.

As discussed earlier in this chapter, different students will approach the same task in different ways. Sometimes an essay title will specify broad organisational requirements. For example, in B above, you are asked to 'outline the arguments for and against' the proposition. However, you might decide either to look at all the 'for' arguments in the first half of the essay and all the 'against' arguments in the second half, or, alternatively, to examine the proposition from both angles with reference to a series of different areas of education. In other essays, you may have more leeway. One common approach is to examine different positions one by one, finally making a case for the one which the majority of the evidence seems to support. Another approach is to make a strong case for one particular position right from the start, while acknowledging and examining alternative (but in your view, weaker) viewpoints along the way.

Top tips

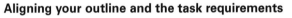

Aligning your outline and the task requirements

When your outline is well developed, go back to your initial analysis of the task to make sure that you have addressed all the points that you originally highlighted, and that you have achieved the required balance in your response.

CROSS
REFERENCE

Studying for
your Education
Degree,
Chapter 4,
Critical
thinking,
Applying and
developing
your critical
thinking skills;
Chapter 5,
Academic
resources:
technology
and the library,
The university
library

Reading and information gathering

Most academic writing assignments require you to read about a particular topic and use scholarly sources to inform your ideas. A good place to start the reading for an assignment is your lecture notes. These will provide an overview of the topic, and they will probably include links to some relevant literature, such as key chapters from core textbooks, and important journal articles, case studies, official reports etc. At the beginning of your studies, lecturers will tend to direct you to relevant sources in this way, but as you progress through your degree, you will be expected to explore the literature more widely and independently. As you develop these research skills, you will be increasingly assessed on your ability to find and select sources, and to use your critical judgement to assess their relevance and credibility. Lecturers will expect you to refer both to sources which support your position on a topic, and sources which challenge it.

Academic texts can be long and difficult to read because of the technical content, much of which may be new to you. It is essential that you devote enough time to reading, but it is also important that you develop effective reading strategies so that you use that time efficiently. When you approach a book, chapter or journal article, first adopt a 'global' approach, ie identify:

- what you expect to find out from it, and how these things relate to your assignment;

- the main message (the author's purpose in writing), and how this relates to your assignment;

- the main points made by the author(s), and how they relate to the main message of the article, and to your assignment.

As you think about how what you are reading relates to the assignment in hand, you might use highlighting, annotations, or note-taking to reflect this. You should also mark or make a note of parts of the text that you think you may need to read more closely at some stage.

Top tips

Strategies for effective reading

1) Use features such as contents pages, indices, abstracts, introductions and conclusions to help you assess the relevance of a book, chapter or article and find specific content.

2) Note how textbooks and journal articles on a particular topic are interrelated. Important books and articles are likely to be referenced by other scholars, and your initial reading may provide links to other sources that could be useful for your essay. This becomes more important as you progress in your studies.

3) You are likely to encounter unknown words in academic reading. Some of these might be subject-related technical terms, such as 'dyslexia' or 'digraph', which you should familiarise yourself with; others may be formal words which are uncommon outside academic writing, such as 'analogous' or 'dichotomy'. If English is not your first language, there may be quite a number of words which are new to you. There is a limited amount of time you can spend reading, so you need to make decisions about how much time to spend investigating unknown non-technical words. Looking up every word you don't know will eat into your reading time and disrupt the reading process. What's more, it is unlikely that you will be able to remember all of these words in the future. Try using these two questions to determine whether or not you should look up a word:

   - Does the word prevent you from understanding the general meaning?

   - Is the word repeated a lot in this text or related texts?

   If the answer to these questions is no, then attempt to guess the word using the context to help you, and read on; if the answer is yes, look up the word.

4) As you take notes, take care to make a note of the reference, including page numbers. It will waste a lot of time if you have to wade through all your sources again when you are compiling your list of references.

CROSS REFERENCE

Studying for your Education Degree, Chapter 4, Critical thinking, Active reading

CROSS REFERENCE

Chapter 3, Referring to sources

5) Try to paraphrase, ie take notes *in your own words*. This will benefit you in these ways:

- as you strive to express ideas in your own way, you will process them and get a good sense of how well you understand what you are reading;

- if you express things in your own words from the start, there is less risk of plagiarism in the final version of your assignment.

Advanced skills

Understanding research article introductions: the CARS model

You will be expected to read and refer to research articles throughout your studies, but as you progress, you will be increasingly expected to take the initiative in finding and selecting particular articles that are relevant to your assignments. The first thing you should look at when considering an article is the **abstract**. This will give you a good idea of whether the article is useful and relevant. If you then decide that you want to find out more, you should begin by looking closely at the **introduction**. This will be easier if you know what to look for. Article introductions typically move through a series of rhetorical stages, or 'moves', ie parts of a text designed to have a particular effect; this is known as the CARS (Creating a Research Space) model (Swales, 1990, p 141).

- **Move 1** involves 'establishing a territory', ie showing that the research area is central or important. This is often achieved through a review of items of previous research in the area.

- **Move 2** involves 'establishing a niche', ie establishing an individual position in relation to the research previously conducted. This often means indicating a 'gap' in the research, by raising questions about or seeking to extend current knowledge in some way.

CROSS
REFERENCE

*Studying for
your Education
Degree,*
Chapter 3,
Becoming
a member
of your
academic and
professional
community,
Academic
phrasebank

- **Move 3** involves 'occupying the niche'. This can be by outlining the nature or purposes of the current research, announcing principal findings, and/or indicating the structure of the paper.

Awareness of the CARS model, and other typical rhetorical patterns, can help you to read and understand difficult articles. Furthermore, understanding the language associated with these rhetorical features of academic writing can help you develop your own academic writing 'toolkit'. You can find many examples of useful phrases which 'move a text forward' in the Academic Phrasebank:

www.phrasebank.manchester.ac.uk/

Writing essentials

There are three things which are especially important in academic writing.

1) **Relevance.** Be sure to make everything you write relevant to the task or question. If the relevance of a point is not immediately clear, then try to make it clear; if you cannot make it clear, leave it out. You will usually have a strict word count, so it is vital not to waste words on irrelevant material which cannot contribute to your mark.

2) **Coherence.** Lecturers often comment on the need for a piece of writing to be 'coherent', or deduct marks for 'lack of coherence'. To be coherent, a piece of writing must **make sense** to the reader. Coherence is tied up with issues discussed earlier, such as having a clear purpose and direction, and writing with a target reader in mind. It is also defined by clear organisation and expression. Coherent texts are *crafted*: they need careful planning and editing. The concept of coherence is examined in detail in Chapter 2.

3) **Criticality.** Most academic writing is 'critical' writing, ie it is analytical and evaluative, rather than just descriptive. This will be discussed below and in other chapters.

CROSS REFERENCE

Chapter 2, Coherent texts and arguments

CROSS REFERENCE

Chapter 2, Coherent texts and arguments, Developing a coherent argument and expressing criticality

Writing critically

A basic requirement in assignments is to make it clear that you have understood important concepts, theories and arguments. In your first year of study, this level of intellectual engagement and understanding is sufficient to pass an assignment. However, as you progress through your educational studies, you will be increasingly assessed on your ability to demonstrate that you have approached concepts, theories, arguments etc *critically*.

Stance

Criticality is related to the idea of having a clear **voice** (Argent, 2017). This means having something to say, and being in possession of an independent viewpoint or perspective on a given topic. In the academic world, this is known as your **stance**, ie, your position in relation to the topic (what *you* think about it) and to the reader (what you want *them* to think about it). There are two questions to consider:

CROSS REFERENCE

Chapter 3, Referring to sources

1) How can you explain your stance?

2) How can you justify your stance and persuade the reader that your stance is valid?

Consider the following essay title:

Discuss the importance of practical work in the development of children's understanding of mathematical concepts.

Many people would be prepared to offer an opinion on this topic without thinking about it too much: 'I suppose we all learn better when we engage in practical activities'; 'In my experience, what is important is that you learn things by heart rather than playing about with counters.' Or they may be reluctant to voice an opinion: 'It's not something I've really thought about.' But your lecturers are not looking for this kind of response; they are interested in a viewpoint that emerges from your *critical engagement* with information, evidence, ideas and debate in academic literature, in this case, the literature dedicated to the issue of practical work in mathematics. *After carefully analysing and evaluating the literature*, you may come to the conclusion that a) practical work is of immense value in developing children's understanding of mathematical concepts; b) practical work has little impact on children's understanding of mathematical concepts; c) practical work may have some value, but other factors may impact equally or more – you may perhaps remain undecided in the face of conflicting evidence. These thoughtful conclusions are very different from the casual opinions stated at the beginning of this paragraph.

Argument

To explain and justify your stance to the reader, you need to present an **argument**. An argument is a way of organising and expressing a viewpoint. It involves a process of **reasoning**, and, to be valid in the academic world, it must be based on solid, convincing **evidence**. This will partly emerge from your analysis and evaluation of the stance, arguments and conclusions of other scholars, and of the evidence they use as support, according to objective criteria (Is the argument logical? Does it lead logically to their conclusions? Is the evidence sound? Does it support their claims?). You will need to compare alternative viewpoints and judge them according to the same criteria. It is on the basis of this analysis and evaluation that you will decide whether to accept the arguments, treat them with caution, or reject them. Your own argument can also be based on a more direct assessment of evidence. For example, you might look at a study on the impact of practical work on children's mathematical understanding in Sweden. You may decide that the findings and conclusions are convincing and widely applicable, or you may judge that the study is too small to be significant, or that it is only relevant to a particular social or national context.

It is not sufficient to look at facts, ideas and issues in isolation. You must demonstrate a good understanding of how these things interrelate. For example, you might compare and contrast several studies on the impact of practical work on children's mathematical understanding to determine if their findings are similar. If they are, this could provide powerful evidence to support a particular argument. If there are differences, you should try to find possible reasons for the differences. Could it be down to the different methodologies used, or are there other variables (eg age, gender, social context) which need to be taken into account? How do these facts impact on your own position?

Nuance

Students sometimes lack confidence in expressing their viewpoint in case it is 'wrong'. But your viewpoint is as valid as anyone else's, so long as it is supported with reasoned argument and sound evidence. However, being confident in your stance does not mean being rigid or close-minded. In fact, your stance should be **nuanced**. This means acknowledging strengths, weaknesses and grey areas. It entails, for example, sometimes *qualifying* your arguments or introducing *caveats* ('practical work is important in developing mathematical understanding *but* only if teachers plan carefully and do not simply allow children to play in an unstructured way'), or taking account of small but important differences in perspective (studies might have similar findings but interpret them in slightly different ways; two scholars may broadly agree that practical work is important in developing mathematical understanding, but have different ideas on how it should be used). A nuanced stance shows that you have been circumspect in your investigation and that you have not rushed to judgement. You must also be sure to recognise any limitations with regard to your own evidence, arguments or conclusions, and to clarify your position regarding which issues can be said to be resolved, and which remain open to debate.

Nuance is very important in education essays which involve an examination of professional ethics and values. These are obviously complex issues, and it is expected that this complexity will be reflected in your discussion.

Expressing stance

Stance is conveyed through the way you treat your content, and through the way you organise and express your ideas. There are particular language features associated with the expression of stance (Biber, 2006; Argent, 2017). This will be explored through the task below, and in Chapter 2, where the organisation and expression of argument is explored in further detail.

CROSS REFERENCE

Chapter 2, Coherent texts and arguments, Developing a coherent argument and expressing criticality

---

Task

Writing critically

How is stance conveyed in the typical examples of student writing below? (Consider, for example, how the writers signal their analysis, evaluation, reasoning, interpretations, feelings and attitude.)

A

Recent research on oracy in schools (for example, Woolley, 2014) has often focused on listening. According to Allott and Waugh (2016), teachers need to model active listening. Too often when a child says something, the teacher's mind is already moving on to the next question or is half distracted by what others in the class are doing. It is important to look interested – and also to *be* interested. Allott and Waugh (2016) maintain that 'if we take time to listen carefully, we will hear fascinating ideas and insights into children's views of the world every day. We will also gain valuable understanding of children's learning, including gaps and misconceptions' (p 53). So while it might seem difficult to give real time and attention to what children are saying when there is so much to fit in to the busy school day and when the needs of the rest of the class also have to be considered, it is essential to establish

13

what Allott and Waugh (2016, p 53) describe as 'an ethos of respectful and careful consideration of everyone's contributions to talk', and this can only be achieved if teachers provide good models of active listening.

B

One important element of communication in education is *active listening*, whereby teachers fully concentrate on and reflect on what pupils say (Jagger, 2015). According to Mobley (2005), active listening is an effective way of signalling empathy, as it conveys to an individual that they have the full attention of the person they are talking to. One aspect of active listening is verbal communication on the part of the listener, such as restating and summarising the speaker's message (Jagger, 2015). Another important element of active listening is non-verbal communication. It is widely held that words form only a minor percentage of communication (Hargie et al, 2004; Sherman, 1993), and that a large part of any message is conveyed through 'paralanguage', such as tone of voice and intonation, and body language, such as posture, eye contact, facial expressions, gestures and touch (Argyle, 1988). This fact impacts considerably on the active listener, who has to be aware not only of the message conveyed through their own non-verbal communication, but also of any non-verbal cues from the speaker: 'One sigh may be communicating a lifetime of emotions' (Freshwater, 2003, p 93).

Discussion: writing critically

In these texts, examples of reasoning include:

- discussion of conditionality/cause and effect

'If we take time to listen carefully, we will hear fascinating ideas and insights into children's views of the world every day. We will also gain valuable understanding of children's learning, including gaps and misconceptions'

- giving reasons for something

Active listening is an effective way of signalling empathy, **as** it conveys to an individual that they have the full attention of the person they are talking to.

- exemplifying and explaining (at the end of the first example the dash and at the end of the second example the colon introduce an elaboration or emphasis of the point):

Too often when a child says something, the teacher's mind is already moving on to the next question or is half distracted by what others in the class are doing. It is important to look interested – and also to *be* interested.

This fact impacts considerably on the active listener, who not only has to be aware of the message conveyed through their own non-verbal communication, but also of any non-verbal clues from the speaker: 'One sigh may be communicating a lifetime of emotions' (Freshwater, 2003, p 93).

Analysis involves identifying relationships or patterns in the literature. This can be implicit in the organisation of ideas. In A, for example, notice how the writer, rather than just describing what each source says, uses his sources to exemplify a 'pattern' he/she has identified.

> Recent research on oracy in schools (for example, Woolley, 2014) has often focused on listening. According to Allott and Waugh (2016), teachers need to model active listening. Too often when a child says something, the teacher's mind is already moving on to the next question or is half distracted by what others in the class are doing.

CROSS REFERENCE

Chapter 3, Referring to sources

Much analysis of the literature involves this 'drawing together' of ideas to provide a context for an essay, article or chapter, as in the example below:

> Throughout the period, research into language in the classroom was continuing, increasing understanding of how talk works in schools and beginning to show evidence of the impact of high-quality classroom talk on attainment (Mercer and Dawes, 2014). In recent years Robin Alexander's (2001) major cross-cultural study comparing education in five countries led to his influential dialogic teaching initiative, which focused on improving language for learning. The Bercow Report (2008) and the resulting Better Communication Research Project focused on children with speech and language communication needs. In 2010 the government appointed Jean Gross as children's Communication Champion to identify and promote good practice. However, all these very positive developments were taking place against a background of growing concern about children's language skills, exemplified by reports such as I CAN's The Cost to the Nation of Children's Poor Communication (2006), and the spread of new ideas and approaches has been patchy, with implementation more difficult than might have been thought.
>
> (Allott and Waugh, 2018)

The texts in the task also include:

- language which indicates the writer's interpretation of or relationship with information and ideas in the literature ('has often focused on'; 'it is widely held that'; 'according to', which suggests a neutral stance towards the idea; 'while it might seem', which suggests a cautious stance);
- language which suggests the writer holds a certain attitude towards information or ideas, and wishes to evoke a particular response in the reader ('too often', 'it is essential', 'important', 'considerably', and, in the Allott and Waugh extract above, 'growing concern').

Stance can also be more subtly conveyed: the 'not only x but y' structure in Example B serves to indicate to the reader that the writer has identified 'y' (underlined) as the most important thing to focus on:

> This fact impacts considerably on the active listener, who has to be aware **not only** of the message conveyed through their own non-verbal communication, **but also** of any <u>non-verbal cues</u> from the speaker

Top tips

Summarising your argument

One way of developing and testing your stance is to see if you can write a single-sentence statement which you think summarises your argument. You can return to this statement as you read and write, and adapt it if necessary to reflect your changing thought processes. You may find that the final form of your statement ultimately forms part of your conclusion.

Task

Summarising your argument

Which of these statements represent **valid arguments** for the essay titles given below?

A

Given the many factors that might influence the emotional well-being of children, consider the question: 'Can teachers really influence the emotional well-being of others?'

Statement 1

Teachers can influence the emotional well-being of children to some extent, but certain other factors such as home background, diet and socio-economic status tend to have a more significant impact.

Statement 2

It is not up to teachers to attend to the emotional well-being of children. That is the responsibility of parents.

Statement 3

Teachers should do more to support the emotional well-being of children.

Statement 4

There are many factors which influence the emotional well-being of children, but teachers are in a prime position to make the most significant impact on the emotional well-being of children.

B

'The core skill of teaching is the ability to communicate.' Using appropriate evidence, explore the arguments for and against this proposition.

Statement 1

Teachers need to improve their communication skills as communication is the core skill of teaching.

Statement 2

Communication is important but it is just one of many skills which are key to teaching, some others being pedagogical skills and classroom management.

Statement 3

Teachers require a variety of skills in their work, but the ability to communicate is the most important.

Statement 4

Teachers need a range of skills, including pedagogical skills and communication skills.

Discussion: summarising your argument

- Regarding Essay A, statements 1 and 4 are both valid arguments, as they recognise the premise that there are many factors influencing the emotional well-being of children, while also reflecting the emphasis in the essay title on the particular role of teachers. They convey different points of view, or stances, on how influential that role is (ie they have different interpretations of the literature, which they will need to justify), but this is to be expected. Statements 2 and 3 are just rather rash personal opinions, only loosely connected to the essay task.

- Regarding Essay B, statements 2 and 3 relate directly to the essay task, reflecting its clear focus on communication skills, even though they disagree on the relative importance of communication skills in comparison with other skills. Statements 1 and 4 are superficially related to the essay task, but they do not reflect the coverage or balance required.

The importance of evidence

To write critically, you need to be objective and able to distinguish between what is fact and what is theory. The more factual evidence you can collect to support theories, the sounder the arguments you will be able to make. For instance, we cannot be absolutely certain that teaching phonics is the best way to introduce young children to reading, but there is much evidence to suggest that it is. You are entitled to have your own opinions, and you will not necessarily fail for disagreeing with current thinking (or, indeed, disagreeing with the views of your lecturers). However, you will almost certainly fail if you do not provide sufficient evidence (in the form of references) to back up your views.

The examples below contrast vague, overgeneralised or unsubstantiated statements with evidence-based claims.

Teachers **are** generally happy with their pay and conditions. ✗

A recent report (Department for Education, 2016) **suggests that** teachers are generally happy with their pay and conditions. ✓

It is a fact that children who don't receive formal phonics instruction fail to learn to read. ✗

Recent evidence (eg Johnston and Watson, 2007) **suggests that** children who learn phonics tend to learn to read more quickly. ✓

> Research **has proved that** phonics is a better approach to early reading than a whole word method. ✗

> Research **indicates that** phonics is a better approach to early reading than a whole word method (Johnston and Watson, 2007). ✓

You can provide balanced arguments by comparing and contrasting evidence from different sources.

> There is evidence to support the efficacy of a systematic synthetic phonics approach. Davis (2013), **however**, while not opposing the teaching of letter–sound correspondences, blending and other phonics skills, maintains that this should be done in the context of reading for meaning.

> **Despite** government figures which suggest that education funding is at the highest level it has been since records began in the mid-1950s, Smith (2018) **maintains** that education is grossly under-funded.

> **On the one hand**, England performs well in reading and literacy achievement of 9- to 10-year-olds compared with other countries in primary literacy (PIRLS, 2011). **On the other hand**, low-attaining pupils in England scored less well than the low-attaining pupils in other countries (Higgins, 2013).

Remember that not all evidence is equal. Be prepared to acknowledge when evidence is absent, unclear, contradictory, or not relevant to the current context.

Top tips

Putting ideas 'in the dock'

Try to think of academic arguments as a court case. You are a member of the jury and, before you make up your mind, you must listen to both the 'defence' (the arguments for) and the 'prosecution' (the arguments against). Hopefully, you wouldn't convict someone of a crime before listening to both sides and seeing what evidence is presented, so why believe unconditionally what academics have to say?

Writing essays

CROSS REFERENCE

Chapter 4, Language in use, Academic style

A critical essay is an in-depth exploration of a topic written in a formal style. The starting point for an essay may be a question for you to answer or a proposition for you to evaluate. Compare:

How important is it for teachers to possess good communication skills?

'The core skill of teaching is the ability to communicate.' Using appropriate evidence, explore the arguments for and against this proposition.

Essays involve discussion of theories and concepts which are key to your development as an educator, and they often provide an opportunity for you to apply these theories or concepts to a real-world educational context.

Essay structure

Good essays have a structure to them – in simple terms, they have a **beginning**, a **middle** and an **end**. This resembles the narrative structure of novels and films, and in many ways, an essay is the 'story' of your investigation of a topic.

Introduction (the 'beginning')

The introduction 'sets the scene' of the essay, telling the reader what you are writing about and why it is important. In this section, you should explain how you propose to achieve your purpose in writing, ie how you will tackle the requirements of the essay title or question. You should provide some background information and outline the main concepts under discussion (providing clarifications and/or definitions if necessary). You should also include a brief outline which indicates the structure of the essay. The outline should reflect the actual ordering of information in the essay and relate directly to any headings and subheadings. This will help to make sure that you stick to the task in hand, and it will ultimately help the reader to navigate your essay. Aim to use approximately 20 to 25 per cent of your word limit for the introduction.

CROSS REFERENCE

Appendix 4, Academic levels at university; Chapter 2, Coherent texts and arguments, Writing essay introductions and conclusions

Main body of the text (the 'middle')

This part should form the bulk of your essay – as much as 60 to 70 per cent of your word count. It can be written as one large section, but the reader must be able to discern blocks of content relating to each subsection mentioned in your introductory outline (and smaller sections within this). You might find it useful to divide the text using appropriate subheadings. (Your department may have particular requirements with regard to this, so always check the assessment guidelines.) In the main body, you must meet the requirements of the essay title or question, according to the academic level you are expected to be at. So, for example, if you are asked to write a second-year (Level 5; Level 8 in Scotland) essay about the importance of practical work in the development of children's understanding of mathematical concepts (discussed earlier in this chapter), you will need to explore the arguments for and against practical work in this area. As many points of view as you can obtain must be taken into account, even if you don't agree with them – you are aiming to be as objective as possible.

Summary and/or conclusion (the 'end')

Summaries and conclusions shouldn't be more than about 10 to 15 per cent of your word limit. A summary expresses the main points of your essay in one or two paragraphs. It is not always necessary to have one, but it can be especially useful in longer (3,500+ word) essays. A conclusion usually refers the reader back to the introduction, to show you have achieved your stated purpose. It draws together the main points discussed in the body of the essay, and reiterates your stance. A conclusion allows you to make some decisions about the topic under discussion. At Level 5, for example, you have three options when concluding (as discussed earlier in this chapter): (i) you can come down in favour of the arguments for the issue being discussed ('practical work is important in the development of children's understanding of mathematical concepts'); (ii) you can come down in favour of the arguments against the issue ('practical work in mathematics is a waste of time'); or (iii) you can be a 'fence-sitter' and remain undecided in the face of conflicting evidence. All three options are equally acceptable, so long as your decision is backed up by appropriate evidence.

A **coherent** essay contains arguments which fit your position and lead naturally to your conclusion.

Reflective essays

CROSS REFERENCE

Studying for your Education Degree, Chapter 3, Becoming a member of your academic and professional community, The teaching community

A reflective essay, as the name suggests, is based on **reflection**. Reflection is the critical analysis of a situation or event, and of your own experience, perceptions, behaviour and thought processes. It can involve analysing situations and events that go well, or not so well. It is a way of making sense of your experience, and relating it to your wider studies and professional development, establishing meaningful connections between theory and practice. It is essential to the development of your knowledge, understanding and intellectual development. Reflection provides an opportunity to think deeply about your beliefs and attitudes, and to explore the values which underpin educational practice.

Reflective practice, the process whereby you stop and think about what you are doing on a day-to-day basis, is central to teaching. It facilitates continuous learning in what is an ever-changing context. Tripp and Rich define reflection as 'a self-critical, investigative process wherein teachers consider the effect of their pedagogical decisions on their situated practice with the aims of improving those practices' (2012, p 678).

CROSS REFERENCE

Studying for your Education Degree, Chapter 4, Critical thinking, Critical thinking in education practice

Reflective essays revolve around an account of a particular event or experience in your practice, something that, on reflection, you view as a **learning experience**. This is known as reflection *on* action, ie looking back at something that has passed, as opposed to reflection *in* action, ie thinking about your current action (Schön, 1987) – though both are important in teaching.

Reflective essays are usually based on **reflective models**. One of the most well known of these consists of three simple questions (Borton, 1970):

- What?
- So what?
- Now what?

Another widely used model is Gibbs' Reflective Cycle (see Figure 1.1).

These reflective models provide a natural structure for a reflective essay.

- They first focus your thoughts on **what happened**, how you perceived an event or experience, and how you felt about it (Borton's 'What?'; Gibbs' 'description' and 'feelings'). This event or experience is commonly known as a **critical incident**, ie something that impacts on you in a significant way, either positively or negatively. Obvious critical incidents in life include the death of a loved one or the birth of your first child, but they can also be something more mundane (though still

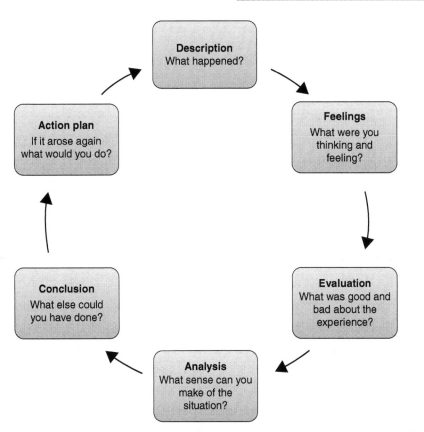

Figure 1.1: Gibbs' Reflective Cycle (adapted from Gibbs, 1988, p 50)

important in terms of your personal and professional development), like a difficult encounter with a colleague, parent or pupil.

- The models then focus on the **meaning** of the critical incident (Borton's 'So what?; Gibbs' 'evaluation' and 'analysis'). Your critical analysis and evaluation of your experience should be informed by the literature, which can help you make sense of the issues which arise. So if, for example, you are writing a reflective essay on the first time you taught a child who spoke little or no English, you would probably want to explore your concerns about the anxieties the child might feel, your concerns about dealing with parents, and so on. To do this, you might examine the literature on English as an Additional Language (EAL). Bear in mind, however, that you would be looking at the literature not just to describe educational practices, but to compare and contrast your experiences with those of others, and to find ways of overcoming the concerns you have.

- The final consideration covered by the models is **action**, ie how different courses of action might have played out, what you might do if a similar situation arose in the future (Borton's 'Now what?'; Gibbs' 'conclusion' and 'action plan'). This comprises an assessment of the impact the experience has had on your understanding and future practice, detailing any insights you have gained, and any actions you need to take in order to enhance your personal development or professional practice.

You might find that you are provided with a template by your programme or module lecturers to help you reflect, based on the above models. Alternatively, you might find it helpful to create a template of your own, perhaps based on a reflective model you like.

Reflective essays are, like other essays, formal in style. However, check assessment guidelines for information on, for example, the use of tenses and personal pronouns. You will usually need to use a range of tenses, for example, the past tense to describe the incident, the present to discuss your current beliefs, and the future to report future planned action. It is also often necessary or natural to use personal pronouns in a reflective essay, eg:

> I noted that the child was reluctant to play with other children.

> I reported the incident to my mentor.

However, where personal pronouns are rather 'chatty', and are easily replaced, it is better to avoid them, eg:

> I thought the child was asleep. ✗

> The child appeared to be asleep. ✓

> I know I need to find out more about EAL. ✗

> It is clear that I need to find out more about EAL. ✓

Top tips

Writing reflectively

1) Reflections are personal, but try to put some distance between you and the critical incident so that you can evaluate it as objectively as possible. Your objectivity should be reflected in your tone, which should be calm, restrained, and factual, eg 'the teacher confronted the parent and this made the other staff uneasy' rather than 'the teacher went for the parent, making everyone not want to be there'.

2) Don't make assumptions and be cautious in your assessments. It is difficult to judge a situation when you have limited information. You cannot usually be sure why someone is behaving in a particular way, but you can speculate, eg 'she *seemed* anxious, *perhaps* because she was uncomfortable with the situation'.

3) Do not confuse your perception with fact, eg 'she *came across as* a bully' rather than 'she *is* a bully'; 'he *appeared to have* ADHD' rather than 'he *clearly had* ADHD'.

4) Be respectful in the way you refer to people, eg 'an *elderly* grandparent' rather than 'an *old* grandparent'; 'a young child with suspected dyslexia' rather than 'a dyslexic girl'.

5) Anonymise participants. This can be done by using official titles ('the phase leader') or pseudonyms.

Task

Reflective essays

Which section of a reflective essay do you think the following extracts come from? What tells you this? Can you relate them to the reflective models discussed above?

A

Jack B (a pseudonym), a six-year-old who is a reluctant reader, struggled to concentrate during quiet reading sessions and was often disruptive. When this was discussed at parents' evening his mother was quite upset. She said that she would like to help, but was not sure how.

B

Seeing Mrs B upset made me anxious as this was my first parents' evening and the class teacher had left me to see a group of parents while she talked to others, as she felt this would be good practice for me for when I had my own class. I was unsure how to react when Mrs B began to cry and told me that she was going through a messy divorce, and that she was finding it difficult to cope with Jack's behaviour, let alone help him with what she referred to as 'schoolwork'.

C

Later, I discussed things with my mentor, who advised me that it was important to develop a dialogue with Mrs B for Jack's benefit. She suggested that I invite her to come into school early the following Tuesday when she came to collect Jack from after-school club. My mentor showed me some simple booklets the literacy coordinator had produced for parents to provide guidance on supporting children with reading. There was a strong emphasis on reading to and with children, and creating a pleasant atmosphere and environment so that reading became a social activity. She suggested that I look through one of the leaflets with Mrs B and talk about ways in which she could help Jack.

D

Following my mentor's advice, I contacted Mrs B and set up a meeting. I brought along some books which I thought would appeal to Jack and talked about things Mrs B could do to engage his interest. We discussed finding a comfortable place to sit with the television off and no distractions, and perhaps making Jack's favourite drink, hot chocolate, so that he would associate reading with things he liked. Mrs B said that she had always loved having bedtime stories when she was a child and she really wanted Jack to enjoy them too, but he found it difficult to settle and wanted to play with his electronic games console instead. We discussed rationing the time he spent playing computer games and not allowing him to have his console in his bedroom. Mrs B thought that might lead to tantrums, but she was willing to give it a try. She thought that after the trauma of his father leaving, Jack needed some undivided attention from her and promised to try that evening and to keep in touch to let me know how things were going.

I now need to explore more strategies for supporting parents with home reading and will also ensure that I talk with Jack about some of the stories his mother will be reading with him.

Writing short reflections for journals or portfolios

You will usually be required to submit short written reflections (approximately 300–500 words) on your teaching placement (distinct from the 'reflective essay' discussed previously in this chapter). These written reflections are also key to **professional portfolio** development for trainee teachers and practitioners alike, so writing in this way is a skill you will need to take with you when qualified. Reflective writing is usually required throughout a school placement, perhaps via a **reflective diary** (also known as a **reflective journal** or **reflective log**) that requires regular entries.

As with a reflective essay, a mixture of tenses is used as you move between past, present and future. However, in contrast to an essay, the writing style used in reflective accounts in journals or for portfolios can be relatively conversational, and the first person pronoun ('I') is almost always used.

Task

Reflective writing

1) Look at the piece of reflective writing below. What do you notice about the following?

- the style of writing;
- the use of tenses;
- the relation to the reflective models (Borton, Gibbs) discussed in the previous section.

In a Year Four class, I went to talk to a boy because he looked like he was upset. I asked him his name but he just ignored me and then said 'Get lost'. He was the same when the other children came up to him. It upset me a bit but I wondered if everything was OK with him so I asked my mentor. She explained that his mum was in hospital having tests and that this sort of behaviour was common in children who are worried and that I shouldn't take anything personally. I did some reading on children in difficult situations before I saw this class again, and it made me understand why he might be behaving in the way he was. I will talk to the mentor tomorrow to see if she has any tips or advice on how I might be able to communicate with him better.

2) Compare the two reflections, A and B, below. What are the main differences? Which one is not acceptable and why?

A

I had real difficulties in Class 3 at Borchester Green School because the class teacher Mrs Perks was a bully. She treated the mother of Annie Lawrence, a pupil with hearing and learning difficulties, appallingly, asking her to leave on several occasions when Mrs Lawrence had come into the classroom with concerns at the end of the day. Michael and Katie, the other teachers in the year group with me, agreed that she was a bully, but Michael said there's usually a reason why people are bullies, so perhaps Mrs Perks was having a bad time. He thought her marriage was breaking up.

I contacted Sharon, the school placement tutor on our course. She then told Mrs Perks, which really scared me and Michael and Katie as I thought we'd all be in trouble. We weren't, and Mrs Perks was actually quite nice, apologising to us.

This whole placement has made me think twice about wanting to carry on teaching.

B

I had real difficulties on my last placement (a Year 3 class) because one of the senior members of teaching staff came across as a bully. There was a particular incident with the mother of a little girl with hearing and learning difficulties that really upset me. Two other students who were on duty with me also thought that the senior member of staff was 'difficult'.

I contacted the school practice tutor and my academic adviser at uni and explained how we all felt. The tutor went and spoke to the senior member of staff in confidence, and she asked if she might meet us with the tutor. The tutor and my academic supervisor reassured us we wouldn't be in trouble, and although the meeting was quite scary for us students, they were right. The senior member of staff apologised profusely, saying both her parents had recently been diagnosed with dementia and she was very stressed. She also explained that she'd been having difficulties with the pupil's mother, because the mother had been subtly threatening and making racist comments to an Asian family with a child in the same class. She said she was sorry that she came across as abrupt, and she thanked us for bringing the issue to her attention. (She also told us that when the tutor had initially raised the matter with her she was shocked that she had come across that way.)

This episode made me realise that I shouldn't judge people immediately and that it's always best to bring concerns to the attention of the appropriate people. I finished the placement some six weeks later thinking it was actually a very good placement for students and that I shouldn't be scared to raise concerns.

Discussion: reflective writing

1) The reflection mostly follows the reflective models (Borton, 1970; Gibbs, 1988) discussed earlier in the chapter: the writer describes the critical incident, and her feelings about it, and there is some analysis of the wider issue, ie the reasons behind

the problem; she also describes the action she has taken to help understand the problem better, and indicated future action, ie seeking advice from her mentor. The style is relatively conversational, there are informal expressions ('get lost', 'upset me a bit'), and the first person ('I') is used throughout. However, it is not overly chatty or in any way inappropriate – in fact, it is **restrained** and **thoughtful** ('upset me *a bit*'). The **critical incident** is related **calmly** and **factually**. It is clear that the student has understood the **value of reflection** and the nature of the **learning process**.

The 'narrative' is related in the past tense tense ('I asked', 'she explained'), and future is used for planned action ('I will talk').

2) Reflection A describes a critical incident, but it is related in a rather clumsy, judgemental fashion, and where there should be analysis, there is only really gossip and speculation. The student does not seem to have learned anything useful from the incident, and her conclusion on future action does not seem very measured, or to really be a logical consequence of what has happened.

Reflection A is also clearly problematic in terms of confidentiality because it names the school, a specific member of staff, a pupil and a pupil's relative, as well as some other teachers and the Placement Tutor.

Reflection B is much better. The language used to relate the critical incident is much more **cautious** and **restrained**: 'came across as a bully' rather than 'was a bully'; the choice of the rather diplomatic word 'difficult' and the accompanying use of quotation marks. The analysis of the incident is **calm** and **factual**, and sensible future action has been identified – notice the use of the present tense here, as the actions refer to general behaviour ('I shouldn't'; 'it's always best to') rather than a particular future plan. The participants are not identifiable. They are referred to in a general sense.

Writing in exams

Examinations test your ability to recall information and write under pressure. However, as with any written assignment, you should read the question or task carefully and highlight key words. You can use the exam booklet to jot down basic ideas and outlines, as long as you cross out any rough work before handing it in. In exams, you do not have a lot of time to spend thinking about organisation, expression or presentation, and examiners will take this into account. Nonetheless, whatever you can do to make the examiner's life easier will count in your favour – remember, your exam script may come from the middle of a pile of 200 or more!

Top tips

Exam strategies

- In a long answer, stick to one point per paragraph and leave a line between paragraphs. This will make your exam script easier to read.
- Make your handwriting as clear as possible – you can get no credit for ideas if no one can read them.
- Make it clear which question you are answering.

Assessment task

Answering exam questions

Look at the exam question below and the students' answers. Have they answered the question well? Why/Why not?

'A teacher must demonstrate consistently the positive attitudes, values and behaviour which are expected of pupils.' Discuss how this aspect of the Teachers' Standards can be achieved.

Answer A

Husbands and Pearce (2012) maintained that effective pedagogy depends on behaviour (what teachers do). A teacher must show consistently high expectations of attainment and behaviour which will bring out the best in every child. The teacher should provide a good role model for pupils in standards of personal presentation and organisation, so that pupils will be encouraged to adopt similar standards for themselves. This can be achieved through sound and thorough planning, with resilience and versatility to cope with unexpected situations. Hattie (2012) argued that teachers' beliefs and commitments are the greatest influence on student achievement. Positive attitudes can be demonstrated through conscientious recordkeeping which shows clearly defined learning objectives, and expectations of how every child can achieve these. A teacher should always have a positive and enthusiastic approach to sessions with pupils, so that they will see learning and achievement as desirable; this can be supported by giving lots of positive feedback during lessons, so that all will be encouraged to participate and share ideas. Indeed, the Education Endowment Foundation (EEF) found from its meta-analysis of research that the greatest impact on pupil attainment was achieved through good quality feedback.

Answer B

A teacher should show consistently positive attitudes by taking a positive attitude towards their teaching. They expect their pupils to behave well so they must behave well themselves because that will show pupils how to behave well. If they do not behave well themselves they cannot expect pupils to learn how. Teachers need to have positive values so that they can teach pupils what is right and wrong and they will not learn properly if they are not doing it right. They can achieve this by following all the rules of the school and telling the pupils to keep the rules. They should show positive attitudes by telling the pupils why what they are learning is good.

Discussion: answering exam questions

- Answer A situates the discussion question in a clear context and provides an independent point of view, supported by examples and research, and an appraisal of wider implications.

- Answer B does not answer the question. It states facts without offering any analysis. Many statements are unsubstantiated or purely anecdotal. It meanders from point to point, sometimes with repetition of phrases, and the style is rather informal and chatty.

Writing dissertations

CROSS
REFERENCE

*Studying for
your Education
Degree,*
Chapter 3,
Becoming
a member
of your
academic and
professional
community,
Academic
principles,
pursuits and
practices,
Teaching,
research and
knowledge

A dissertation is a long evidence-based or research-focused essay, usually between 10,000 and 20,000 words. It shares many of the requirements discussed in relation to critical essays, such as having a clear purpose and strategy, a defined target reader, a conventional structure, and a well-developed stance and argument. An **evidence-based** education dissertation could involve conducting your own review of the evidence surrounding a particular educational practice or resource. A **research-focused** dissertation could involve investigation of a current 'knowledge gap' or 'problem' in the field of education. Remember, though, that there are strict ethics codes associated with conducting research, and you may need to seek ethical approval for an empirical study. Your tutors will advise you on procedures.

Before you start your dissertation, you will have to write a **proposal** outlining your chosen line of enquiry. You will need to make it clear that the dissertation is feasible, and that you have the knowledge and skills to carry it out. You will also need to outline any potential challenges or problems you foresee. With research dissertations, you will need to complete the ethics form prescribed by your university. Finally, you will need to include an initial bibliography, ie sources that you think will be of use to you.

Like all essays, dissertations must have a 'beginning', a 'middle' and an 'end'. An **introduction** provides background information on the topic under review, or the gap or problem under investigation. The introduction also presents the rationale for your current review or investigation, and outlines how you intend to go about your study. A **conclusion** serves to draw everything together with a summary of the main argument and its implications for teaching practice.

The 'middle' part of a dissertation is founded on an extensive **literature review**, presenting an analysis and evaluation of current scholarship on the topic, and detailing key concepts, theories and arguments.

Research-focused dissertations may adopt the **IMRAD** structure found in many scientific journal articles:

- **I**ntroduction;
- **M**ethod;
- **R**esults;
- **D**iscussion.

With this structure, the introduction and literature review comprise a single section, though they are sometimes separated. Your **methodology** describes the type of study you are conducting (quantitative, qualitative, mixed methods), and your methods of data collection and analysis (eg a survey, statistical analysis). It also covers any ethical considerations. The **results** section details the findings of your study; tables and figures are often useful tools in this section. The **discussion** section is where you interpret your findings and discuss their meaning and significance. This will involve relating what you have found out to current knowledge in the field, and highlighting any new insights or understanding. Sometimes in education, hypothetical research is proposed, in which case only the methodology section is included. The 'discussion' section then might be around the potential pitfalls in carrying out the research.

Dissertations also have an **abstract**, which comprises a short summary of the whole dissertation, and a list of **references**.

CROSS
REFERENCE

*Studying for
your Education
Degree,*
Chapter 3,
Becoming
a member
of your
academic and
professional
community,
Advanced
skills,
Research
reports

Summary

This chapter has introduced the topic of academic writing. It has explored the context of academic writing at university, and provided guidance on how to approach academic writing tasks in your education degree. It has explored some of the general principles of academic writing, the writing process, and important features of typical text types in education. It has also highlighted the centrality of criticality in writing, something which will be expanded on in subsequent chapters.

Sources of example texts

Allott, K and Waugh, D (2016) *Language and Communication*. London: Sage.

Borton, T (1970) *Reach, Touch and Teach: Student Concerns and Process Education*. London: Hutchinson.

Davis, A (2013) To Read or Not to Read: Decoding Synthetic Phonics. *Impact No. 20*.

Higgins, S (2013) What Can We Learn from Research? In Waugh, D and Neaum, S (eds) *Beyond Early Reading*. Northwich: Critical Publishing.

Johnston, R and Watson, J (2007) *Teaching Synthetic Phonics*. Exeter: Learning Matters.

Mullis, I V S, Martin, M O, Foy, P and Drucker, K T (2012) *The PIRLS 2011 International Results in Reading*. Chestnut Hill, MA: TIMSS & PIRLS International Study Center, Boston College. [online] Available at: http://timss.bc.edu/pirls2011/downloads/P11_IR_FullBook.pdf (accessed 20 July 2012).

Tripp, T and Rich, P (2012) Using Video to Analyse One's Own Teaching. *British Journal of Educational Technology*, 43(4), 678–704.

Woolley, G (2014) *Developing Literacy in the Primary School*. London: Sage.

References

Academic Phrasebank. [online] Available at: www.phrasebank.manchester.ac.uk (accessed 15 February 2017).

Argent, S (2017) The Language of Critical Thinking. [online] Available at: www.baleap. org/event/eap-northcritical-thinking (accessed 27 February 2017).

Biber, D (2006) Stance in Spoken and Written University Registers. *Journal of English for Academic Purposes*, 5(2), 97–116.

Borton, T (1970) *Reach, Touch and Teach: Student Concerns and Process Education*. London: Hutchinson.

Gibbs, G (1988) *Learning by Doing: A Guide to Teaching and Learning Methods*. Oxford: Further Education Unit, Oxford Polytechnic.

Schön, D (1987) *Educating the Reflective Practitioner: Towards a New Design for Teaching and Learning in the Professions*. San Francisco: Jossey-Bass.

Swales, J (1990) *Genre Analysis*. Cambridge: Cambridge University Press.

Swales, J and Feak, C (2012) *Academic Writing for Graduate Students: Essential Tasks and Skills*. 3rd ed. Michigan: Michigan ELT.

Woodford, P (1967) Sounder Thinking Through Clearer Writing. *Science*, 156(3776), 743–45.

Chapter 2
Coherent texts and arguments

Learning outcomes

After reading this chapter you will:

- have gained an understanding of the concept of coherence in writing;

- understand the importance of effective planning;

- understand how to write effective essay introductions and conclusions;

- understand the importance of editing and redrafting your text;

- understand how to develop paragraphs and texts which are easy to follow for the reader;

- understand how to develop coherent arguments;

- be aware of how your choices of grammar and expression can affect meaning, clarity and coherence.

Reflection

1) What do you think it means to write 'coherently'? How do you think this can be achieved?

2) What do you understand by 'a coherent argument'? How is a coherent argument constructed?

3) How do you go about planning a piece of written work? How much time do you spend on this?

4) How do you go about editing a piece of written work? How much time do you spend on this?

If a text is **coherent**, it **makes sense to the reader**. In this chapter, you will analyse a range of academic education texts to help you understand how coherence is achieved. Alongside this, you will develop effective planning, writing and editing strategies so that you are able to produce coherent texts and arguments of your own.

CROSS REFERENCE

Chapter 1, Academic writing: text, process and criticality, Analysing a writing assignment

Planning for coherence

Planning is the process of selecting and organising information and ideas in order to respond to an assignment task effectively. The planning process should start with an examination of the wording of the task or question. This involves analysing or 'unpacking' it so that you can be sure about what the lecturer assessing your work is expecting you to do.

When you are sure you understand what you are being asked to do, you should start to draft a plan or 'outline'.

CROSS
REFERENCE

General and
specific
information

An outline is much more than a mere list of topics; there should be a clear **organising principle**, both for the text as a whole, and for individual sections of the text. This might involve presenting items chronologically, or in order of importance; it often involves starting with general information and moving on to more specific information. Your outline should indicate how individual items relate to the main topic and to each other, ie how they are governed by your main organising principle.

Below are some examples of common organisational frameworks (for a piece of writing, or for sections of a piece of writing) which can help you to organise information and ideas (Jordon, 2001):

- **classification**, ie the division of something into groups, classes, categories etc, usually according to specific criteria;
- **comparison and contrast**, ie an examination of similarities and differences;
- **cause and effect**, ie how one thing influences another; what results from certain situations or actions;
- **problem-solution**, ie the description and analysis of a problem, and the evaluation of possible solutions to that problem.

Other common elements of academic texts include **description**, **narrative**, **definition of key terms**, and **exemplification**. These different elements may overlap: there is likely to be discussion of the causes and effects of a problem; classification may well require discussion of similarities and differences; description, definition of key terms, and exemplification are integral to many organisational frameworks.

Task

Organisational frameworks

1) What organisational principles are being employed in the essay plans below?

A

Factors that might influence a child's reading ability

- reading experiences outside school
- home background
- exposure to songs and rhymes
- hearing stories and sharing books
- parental support and enthusiasm

- ability to distinguish between sounds
- hearing and visual abilities
- attitude of teachers
- culture of school, eg discussing texts, reading stories

B

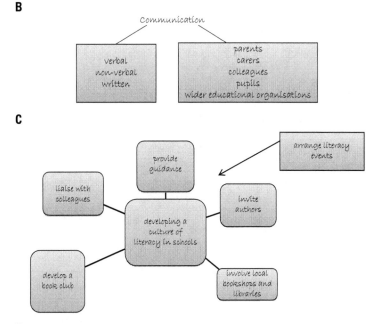

C

D

Parents' and carers' responses to child being diagnosed as on the autism spectrum

- shock and disbelief
- anger and turmoil
- acceptance and resilience

E

- Mature student teachers – valuable life experience; particularly drawn to difficult to recruit areas such as early years and secondary mathematics
- Significant drop in applications from over 25s in primary – loss of bursaries/ introduction of fees?
- Targeted recruitment drive?

F

Should grammar be taught in discrete lessons or as part of reading and writing?

Arguments for grammar as discrete lessons	Arguments for grammar through reading and writing
- Ensures topics are covered - Strong focus on subject knowledge - Exercises can test learning - Published grammar text books can be used systematically - Less pressure on teachers' subject knowledge if they only have to focus on one aspect at a time	- Grammar in context is more meaningful to children - Real examples can be found in texts and discussed - Grammatical features can be incorporated into learning outcomes for writing - Discrete grammar lessons may be dull - Myhill (2012) and Andrews et al (2007) provide evidence in favour

2) Which of the sections below do you think are relevant to the essay provided? How could the relevant sections be effectively organised?

A

Given the many factors that might influence children's well-being, consider the question: 'Can teachers really influence the well-being of others?'

Introduction/background – refer to title

- Factors influencing a child's well-being (home background, environment, lifestyle, socio-economic status, cultural factors, health, learning difficulties)
- Definition of teacher
- Definition of well-being
- Concept of 'empowerment'
- Contextualise to my field of teaching
- Extent to which teachers can influence
- Compare with influence of other professionals, eg health professionals, social workers, school support staff

Conclusion – can have an impact, but other factors (eg home background, environment, lifestyle, socio-economic status, cultural factors, health, learning difficulties) are important too – potential of teachers to influence these things?

B

'The core skill of teaching is the ability to communicate.' Using appropriate evidence, explore the arguments for and against this proposition.

Introduction/background – claimed that communication is the core skill of teaching

- Definition of communication
- Definition of proposition
- Relative importance of (other) different core skills (pedagogic skills, intellectual skills, subject knowledge) – are these less important than communication?

- All teachers should learn a foreign language
- Problems caused by breakdown in communication
- Different types of communication: verbal, written, non-verbal
- How communication impacts on other aspects of teaching – thus more important?
- Different forms of communication: pupils, families, colleagues, partner organisations
- Is communication more of a concern for school managers than classroom teachers?

  Conclusion – teachers need a range of skills but communication is integral to all, and it is very difficult to be a good teacher without good communication skills, even if competent in 'technical' skills

Editing and redrafting for coherence

Editing is a process whereby a writer makes changes to the content, organisation and expression of a text in order to improve it. The writing and editing process is also referred to as 'drafting' and 'redrafting', with writers producing different 'drafts' of a text. (Lecturers may sometimes ask you to submit 'a first draft' – though this does not mean that it should be unedited! It is probably best to think of this as 'an early draft'.)

The truth about writing!

If you lack experience in academic writing, it can sometimes feel as if you are a 'novice', 'outside', looking 'in' on the world of 'expert' writers (academics and experienced student writers), where everyone gets everything right first time. But this is far from the truth! In fact, you are a member of a diverse **writing community**, and members from all levels of this community, including experienced writers, usually have to work very hard to produce text which is clear and coherent. In order to make sure their writing makes sense to the reader, it is usually necessary for most writers to read and edit their text frequently at all stages of the writing process. It is tempting to believe that you will be able to get away with less editing as you become more experienced in writing, but in fact, research suggests that the more experienced a writer becomes, the more they edit and redraft (Benson and Heidish, 1995). If experienced academics see the value and necessity of the editing and redrafting process, then it seems advisable that you, as a developing academic writer, should follow their example.

Putting yourself in the reader's shoes

If you do not read your own text, you cannot imagine the reader's experience as they navigate the text. You should read your text frequently, *putting yourself in the reader's shoes*. As you read, ask yourself the following questions:

- Would this make sense to someone else?

- Are points and ideas organised according to clear principles?
- Are they in a logical order?
- Are the links between them explicit?
- Is there anything which is vague or ambiguous?
- Does the text *flow*?

CROSS
REFERENCE

Chapter 5,
Preparing
your work for
submission

When reading and editing, your focus should be on **meaning**; at a later stage, you will need to proofread your text in order to correct surface errors in grammar and punctuation, but this should not be the focus while you are still at the stage of making decisions about content and organisation. You also need to leave time at the end of the writing process to read through the text several times. Again, you should first focus on meaning (before proofreading). Being able to do this also requires good time management: you can't do it if you finish the essay ten minutes before the deadline!

Task

Editing and redrafting for coherence

Look at the following drafts. Text A is accurate and academic in style, but the lecturer reading it found it a little hard to follow. What changes has the writer made in B in order to make the text more coherent for the reader?

A

Myhill has researched and written about teaching grammar in the context of writing lessons (Myhill et al, 2012). She argues that many children would benefit from an approach which situates learning about it within appropriate writing contexts rather than in separate lessons (Myhill et al, 2012, p 3). The evidence from Myhill and the University of Exeter's Centre for Research in Writing demonstrates that this leads to better writing outcomes. They argue that there are key principles when teaching in this way.

B

Myhill has researched and written on contextualised grammar teaching (Myhill et al, 2012). She argues that many children would benefit from an approach which situates learning about grammar within appropriate writing contexts, 'not as a body of separate knowledge learned for its own sake' (Myhill et al, 2012, p 3). The evidence from Myhill and the University of Exeter's Centre for Research in Writing demonstrates that contextualised approaches lead to better writing outcomes. Myhill and her colleagues argue that there are key principles when teaching grammar in this contextualised way.

Discussion: editing and redrafting for coherence

CROSS
REFERENCE

Cohesion and
paragraph
structure,
Referring
back in
the text,
Repetition,
variation and
pronoun use

Text B is clearer, as it is far more **explicit**.

- It reminds the reader that the topic is *teaching about grammar* rather than just in general by repeating the word 'grammar' at several key points.

- Text B is explicit about the study being referred to, and gives a direct quotation from the text rather than paraphrasing.

- In Text A, the reader is having to guess what 'it' refers to. It is important to be very sure that the reader can trace a pronoun like 'it' or 'they' back to the thing it refers to. This will be discussed later in this chapter.

Writing essay introductions and conclusions

A coherent essay makes things clear for the reader right from the start with a clear **introduction**. The introduction should tell the reader:

- Your purpose in writing. You should refer directly to the essay title or question.

- Some general background information, including the main concepts under discussion, clarifications, definitions etc.

- How you will address the topic in order to achieve your purpose and satisfy the needs and expectations of the reader. You should include a brief overview of what will be included in the essay in order to achieve the stated purpose. The items listed in this overview should reflect the order in which you present them in the essay (and refer to exact subheadings if you have them).

Below is an example introduction for one of the essays referred to earlier in the chapter:

'The core skill of teaching is the ability to communicate.' Using appropriate evidence, explore the arguments for and against this proposition.

> It has been claimed that the core skill of teaching is communication (Allott and Waugh, 2016). It is abundantly clear that communication is important in teaching. Teachers are required to speak to pupils, families and colleagues every day. They must also provide written communications, in the form of pupil records, for example. However, it could be argued that pedagogical skills, intellectual skills, and even general administrative capacity are equally, if not more, important. **The aim of this essay** is to examine the extent to which communication can be considered to be the *core* teaching skill. **It will begin by** examining what is meant by the term 'communication' in teaching. **It will then** outline what are generally considered to be the core skills required by teachers, with reference to the Teachers' Standards (2012). **It will go on** to examine the impact of communication skills on a range of teaching and learning activities, and assess the role that poor communication has played in a number of documented 'failures' in teaching.

Note the key phrases (in **bold**) used to indicate each section of the essay. Notice also the form of the verb that follows these phrases (the aim is *to do*; begin by *doing*; go on *to do*). These types of phrases, used to guide the reader through a

CROSS REFERENCE

Linking ideas

text, are known as **signposts** (discussed later in the chapter). These signposts can be adapted to most essays, and they are a useful tool for ensuring that you have a clear structure. Common verbs for describing what a writer *does* in essays are:

- outline;
- describe;
- identify;
- examine;
- look into;
- analyse;
- evaluate;
- explore.

CROSS REFERENCE

Appendix 3, Key phrases in assignments

These terms are not interchangeable: for example, they can express whether you intend to simply present or describe something, or whether you aim to go deeper. The terms you use should relate to the key terms used in the essay title or question.

Longer essays may have an introduction which provides quite an extended account of the essay context. An example can be seen later in this chapter.

A **conclusion** is the part of the essay where you draw everything together. It usually contains the following:

CROSS REFERENCE

Developing a coherent argument and expressing criticality

- a reference to what was said in the introduction to show that you have achieved your stated purpose;
- a summary of your argument, drawing together the main points discussed in the body of the essay;
- a statement on where you stand on the topic you've discussed, and the significance of this;
- some practical recommendations and/or implications for teaching practice.

Below is an example of a conclusion for the same essay.

> In conclusion, good communication skills lie at the heart of all areas of teaching, and can thus be considered to be at least as important as the pedagogical and intellectual skills that a teacher must be proficient in. It is therefore important that communication skills are developed and assessed as part of teacher education. However, teachers do not function in isolation. As discussion of a number of reported teaching 'failures' in this essay has shown, a breakdown in communication between management and teachers can result in or contribute to problems for pupils. Thus, it is clear that effective communication is something which should be prioritised at all levels of teaching.

Cohesion and paragraph structure

A text is made up of paragraphs. For a text to be clear and coherent, each paragraph must have a clear focus and structure. Good paragraphs usually have the following structural characteristics:

- they deal with a single unified point and do not digress from this;

- they often introduce this point in the first sentence;
- they usually move from general to specific information and ideas;
- they order and connect ideas in a logical manner.

In order for a paragraph to develop clearly, the points or ideas it contains should be linked in *meaningful* ways. This meaningful linking is known as 'cohesion' (Halliday and Hassan, 1976), and it is achieved through organisation, grammar and word choice, aspects of which will be discussed in this section. (Note that the extracts in the following task will be referred to throughout this chapter.)

Task

Cohesion and paragraph structure

Read the paragraphs below.

1) Do you find them easy to read?
2) The paragraphs demonstrate some of the typical features of paragraph development and cohesion in English. Can you identify any aspects of organisation, grammar or word choice which make your life easier as a reader?

Extract A: an extract from a typical student essay

One important element of communication in teaching is *active listening*, whereby teachers fully concentrate on and reflect on what pupils say (Allott and Waugh, 2016). According to Smith (2005), active listening is an effective way of signalling empathy, as it conveys to pupils that they have the full attention of the person they are talking to. One aspect of active listening is verbal communication on the part of the listener, such as restating and summarising the speaker's message (Allott and Waugh, 2016). Another important element of active listening is non-verbal communication. It is widely held that words form only a minor percentage of communication (Hargie et al, 2004; Sherman, 1993), and that a large part of any message is conveyed through 'paralanguage', such as tone of voice and intonation, and body language, such as posture, eye contact, facial expressions, gestures and touch (Argyle, 1988). This fact impacts considerably on the active listener, who not only has to be aware of the message conveyed through their own non-verbal communication, but also of any non-verbal clues from the speaker: 'One sigh may be communicating a lifetime of emotions' (Freshwater, 2003, p 93).

Extract B: an extract from an education textbook (Allott and Waugh, 2016, p 2)

Learning to talk involves different sets of skills and knowledge, which were described in the DfES training materials Communicating Matters (2005) as strands. This way of looking at language is useful in getting to grips with what is involved in language development, and in assessing and supporting that development. The four strands identified are:

1. Knowing and using sounds and signs (phonological development).
2. Knowing and using words (vocabulary development).

3. Structuring language (syntax).

4. Making language work (pragmatics).

Extract C: an extract from an education textbook (Waugh and Neaum, 2013, p 20)

Bunting (2000) maintained that engaging children in activities which require close attention to language may 'contribute to their interest in and ability to use language' (p 101). However, she cautions that this alone is not a justification for exploring language: 'language is interesting in its own right and looking at language should be an everyday part of the work of the classroom' (p 101). Indeed, such work can also be done outside the classroom on literacy walks and language trails.

Extract D: an (adapted) extract from the final section of an education article (Gill and Waugh, 2017, p 42)

Creating an enriching classroom environment, with a focus on supporting the teaching of words with unusual grapheme/phoneme correspondences is important. A working wall, where both adults and pupils can display useful materials, provides a focal point where word groups, learning aids and other resources can be used for reference. Sticky-notes are useful for collecting 'tricky' words, and for highlighting where they can be found in texts and other reading materials. Teaching aids such as word mats and flashcards are invaluable, and many good examples of these can be found online.

General and specific information

As shown in Table 2.1, all the example paragraphs above move from **general** statements to more **specific** information, which is typical of English paragraph structure. General statements at the start of a paragraph often serve to establish the topic of the whole paragraph: these are sometimes called **topic sentences** or **umbrella statements**. As these examples show, specific information can include definitions, explanations, analysis, evidence, evaluation, and exemplification, but this varies depending on the purpose of the writer.

Table 2.1: General and specific content

EXAMPLE TEXT	GENERAL TOPIC	SPECIFIC DETAILS
A	Introduction and definition of key concept/term	Relevance, significance, analysis, evidence
B	General statement/claim	Explanation, categorisation
C	General statement/claim	Analysis, argument
D	Recommendation	Explanation, exemplification, focus on and exemplification of 3 points (word wall, collections of 'tricky' words and teaching aids)

Task

General and specific information

Identify and describe the general and specific information in the paragraph below.

> Children need to be able to hear the separate sounds, or phonemes, in words, and to produce them. English is a phonologically complex language, with (depending a little on regional accents) 20 vowel phonemes, such as /aw/ and /ai/, and 24 consonant phonemes, such as /f/ and /ch/. The consonant phonemes can be combined in 49 different clusters at the beginning or end of syllables, including clusters of three such as the cluster at the beginning of 'straight'. Children take a long time to learn to produce all the English phonemes accurately in all positions in words. Their early speech is full of phonological simplifications such as 'bo' for 'ball', 'guck' for 'duck' and 'bikkit' for 'biscuit'. This can make their speech difficult to understand.
>
> (Allott and Waugh, 2016, p 5)

Old and new information

To respond to an academic assignment, it is necessary to provide the reader with a lot of information. However, it is also necessary to let the reader know how each new piece of information fits in with what has already been said. The example extracts above demonstrate one typical way of doing this in English: they frequently refer back to **'old'** information given in the previous sentence, or earlier in the text, before supplying **'new'** information. It is a way of staying on topic, linking ideas together, and focusing the reader on the new information. This feature is highlighted below, where there is reference back to information and phrases introduced earlier in the text. Sometimes references go back to the main theme introduced in the first sentence; sometimes they refer to something in the previous sentence.

> It is also important to consider **whether or not boys perform as well as girls** in other subjects across the curriculum. Looking at the most recent Trends in International Mathematics and Science Study, the corresponding international tests to the PIRLS, in mathematics **boys marginally outperformed girls** in England, whilst in science **the results were broadly similar**, a pattern which was relatively common across the countries tested (Mullis, Martin, Foy and Hooper, 2016). If it is the case that **boys' attainment is on a par or slightly better than girls** in other subjects, **their relative underperformance** in reading requires further investigation.

Looking specifically at reading for pleasure, Hempel-Jorgensen, Cremin, Harris and Chamberlain (2017) offer two key reasons why boys are positioned in the classroom as struggling readers: teachers' perceptions of children's social and learner identities, and the ways in which teaching practices encourage reading for pleasure. The authors argue that **'boys' (dis)engagement** may not solely be a gender issue and may be related to how they are positioned in **teachers' pedagogy** as a result of **teachers' perceptions** of children's intersecting gender, ethnicity and social class identities' (p 1). **This** is a small-scale study, focusing on just four schools, but it is certainly thought provoking to consider the power of a teacher to influence achievement not only through **teaching practices**, but also through **their own ideas and opinions** on the children they teach.

(Extracts from essay by Tom Maxwell)

Task

Old and new information

Find the parts of the text below which refer back to information given earlier in the text.

Children need to be able to combine words in order to communicate more complex meanings than can be conveyed by single words. They have to learn the rules that govern how words can be combined into sentences; for example, basic word order in English is subject, verb, object (eg The boy ate the apple), but this is not the case in all languages. From single words children start to combine two words, often using words such as 'more' and 'no' in combination with many other words. Utterances become longer and longer, particularly once the word 'and' begins to be used, and grammatical complexity also increases, with a wider range of connectives used to express more sophisticated meanings, and increasing ability to express negatives and ask questions.

(Allott and Waugh, 2016, p 6)

Referring back in the text: repetition, variation and pronoun use

Reference back to information earlier in the text can be achieved through repetition, as demonstrated in Extract A. Students are sometimes reluctant to repeat as they have been told that repetition will bore the reader or will indicate their lack of knowledge or vocabulary. The truth is that there is good and bad repetition: 'bad' repetition involves the inclusion of redundant information or words, or 'clumsy' reiteration of the same word in sequential sentences; 'good' repetition is a vital part of cohesion (Halliday and Hasan, 1976), and, used carefully, it greatly improves the lucidity of the text for the reader. In Extract A on page 39, repetition of the key term reminds the reader what the text is about, and enables them to understand how each new point relates to the central concept in question. Another way of staying on topic is through 'chains' of related words through a text, for example, the use of words related to 'vocabulary' in the following text.

> Bunting (2000) makes numerous suggestions for activities and word games which have the potential to engage children's interest and develop their **vocabularies**. These include exploring **words** from other languages which have become part of the English **lexicon** such as *yoghurt, tobacco, menu, bungalow, anorak* and *mosquito*. To these we might add a number of words which are so commonly used now that many won't be aware that they were unheard of by some of our grandparents. **Names** of foods from other countries, in particular, become common parlance and include: *pizza, pasta, spaghetti, masala, paella, tacos, fajitas, kebab* and *sushi*. By exploring such words, children can begin to understand that grapheme-phoneme correspondences vary around the world and that when learning another language they need to be aware of this.
>
> (Waugh and Neaum, 2013, p 24)

However, caution should be employed when considering the use of **synonyms** (words which have the same or a similar meaning). You should ask yourself if a synonym really has the same meaning as your original word, particularly if you find it in a thesaurus and haven't used it before. If you are unsure, do not be afraid to repeat the original word. In the case of technical terms (such as 'active listening' in Extract A on page 39), you should not usually change these at all ('active hearing' or 'careful listening' are not acceptable because they do not reflect conventional usage in the field).

CROSS REFERENCE

Chapter 4, Language in use, Top tips, Using a thesaurus

Sometimes a noun can be referred back to with a pronoun (*it, them, him, her, them*, etc), eg:

> **Most skilled practitioners** take an eclectic approach: **they** have an awareness of the strengths and weaknesses of the various perspectives and models, and **they** use **their** professional judgement to select a pedagogical approach most suitable for a given set of circumstances.

When deciding whether to repeat a noun or replace it with a pronoun, ask yourself if the reader will easily understand what the pronoun refers to. If there is any doubt, repeat the noun.

Task

Noun or pronoun?

Which choice would help the reader most in the text below? (Remember that one choice can affect the following choice, so there are different ways to make the text coherent. The choices you make are about the whole text, not just one sentence.)

> The National Reading Panel in the USA has summed up (2000) research on vocabulary development by citing nine implications for reading instruction. They suggest that it/vocabulary should be taught in the classroom both directly and indirectly, and that repetition and multiple exposures to new items/vocabulary items is important. Learning in rich contexts is important for learning it/vocabulary, and tasks based on it/vocabulary should be restructured when this is necessary to make meaning clear. Learning it/vocabulary should always entail active involvement in learning tasks, including the use of computer technology to help teach it/vocabulary. It/Vocabulary can also be acquired through incidental learning. Finally the study suggests that it is important to remember that how it/vocabulary is assessed and evaluated can have different effects on instruction, and that dependence on a single method for teaching it/vocabulary will not result in optimal learning.
>
> (Adapted from Waugh and Neaum, 2013)

Referring back in the text: useful words and phrases

There are several examples in the previous texts in this chapter of particular words and phrases commonly used to refer back to 'old' information in the previous sentence:

A

Learning to talk involves different sets of skills and knowledge, which were described in the DfES training materials Communicating Matters (2005) as strands. **This way of looking at language** is useful in getting to grips with what is involved in language development, and in assessing and supporting **that development**.

B

Bunting (2000) makes numerous suggestions for activities and word games which have the potential to engage children's interest and develop their vocabularies. **These** include exploring words from other languages which have become part of the English lexicon such as *yoghurt, tobacco, menu, bungalow, anorak* and *mosquito*. To **these** we might add a number of words which are so commonly used now that many won't be aware that **they** were unheard of by some of our grandparents.

C

Children take a long time to learn to produce all the English pho¬nemes accurately in all positions in words. **Their** early speech is full of phonological simplifications such as 'bo' for 'ball', 'guck' for 'duck' and 'bikkit' for 'biscuit'. **This** can make their speech difficult to understand.

D

Bunting (2000) maintained that engaging children in activities which require close attention to language may 'contribute to their interest in and ability to use language' (p 101). However, she cautions that **this** alone is not a justification for exploring language: 'language is interesting in its own right and looking at language should be an everyday part of the work of the classroom' (p 101). Indeed, **such work** can also be done outside the classroom on literacy walks and language trails.

These words and phrases can play a huge role in helping the reader to follow the development of a text. Common words and phrases used to refer back are: 'this', 'these', 'the' and 'such'. The words 'this' and 'these' can be used alone (as in some of the examples above), but they (and other words) are often followed by a noun which repeats or summarises information given in the previous sentence. Drummond (2016) has identified the most common 'summary nouns' in academic English as:

- time
- case
- point
- view
- period
- process
- approach
- question
- problem
- area.

The following nouns are commonly used in educational writing:

- review
- programme
- unit
- scale
- assignment
- theme
- curriculum
- institution
- survey
- training
- treatment.

These summary nouns have also been called 'signalling nouns' (Flowerdew, 2003), and indeed, writers often choose to refer back to something with a noun which *signals* their own attitude or stance. For example, 'this problem' is subtly different to 'this challenge', the latter possibly signalling a more positive attitude. What's more, the writer might underline their stance by adding an adjective, such as 'serious' or 'minor' before 'problem'. These choices are part of *criticality*, as they convey the writer's interpretation and stance.

CROSS REFERENCE

Developing a coherent argument and expressing criticality

Task

Referring back in the text to summarise and comment

1) How does the writer summarise and signal her attitude to something she refers back to in the text below?

> Recently, basic-skills website featured a summary of a review of the reading research by Torgerson et al (Research Report no. 711). The 85 page document is linked to this summary. It is, in effect, purported to be a reworking of the National Reading Panel's report in the US (2000), or more accurately, the reading committee chair's report of the same data (Ehri et al, 2001). This report was commissioned by the DfES and funded by them. The committee, headed by Professor Greg Brooks, was supported and advised at each stage of the review with helpful comments and suggestions. This is a dense document, with numerous tables and appendices, arcane discussions of statistical minutiae and issues regarding experimental design, etc, all to the end (it appears) of drawing a vague set of conclusions which lead the reader to believe that synthetic phonics programmes have not been proven to be effective beyond other methods by any margin sufficient to be trustworthy. The reality is, that every statement under the heading key findings is incorrect or seriously compromised by the true facts.
>
> (McGuinness, 2006, p 1)

2) In the examples below, link back to the ideas in the first sentence using 'this'/'these' and a word from the lists of common summary nouns given earlier in this chapter.

a) The school was closed down for breaching a number of regulations. This _____ was widely reported in the press.

b) Many parents believed that children were exposed to radical viewpoints. This _____ is now widely contested.

c) Many children receive inadequate nutrition at home. The government needs to tackle this serious _____.

d) Different schools approach phonics in different ways. Whichever _____ is adopted, parents need to be provided with a clear rationale.

e) Truancy can be tackled in a number of ways. Whichever _____ is selected, it is important that parents are fully informed.

f) There is considerable debate about the efficacy of the mastery approach to mathematics. This _____ should be the subject of more extensive research.

3) How do you think the authors of the academic education texts below may have referred back to the ideas in the previous sentences to repeat, summarise or comment on an idea?

a) Bunting (2000) maintained that engaging children in activities which require close attention to language may 'contribute to their interest in and ability to use language' (p 101). However, she cautions that _____ alone is not a justification for exploring language: 'language is interesting in its own right and looking at language should be an everyday part of the work of the classroom' (p 101).

(Waugh and Neaum, 2013, p 20)

b) For example, the NRP combined the data across ages, across types of instruction (single child, small groups, all children in a classroom), across the number of hours of instruction (days, weeks, months), quite apart from the range of programme types they believed fit the designation: 'synthetic' or 'systematic.' _____ included Orton-Gillingham with its emphasis on letter names as well as sounds and a strong focus on memorizing syllable types, onset-rime/analogy programmes, and more bread-and-butter synthetic phonics programmes that were either well thought out or not.

(McGuinness, 2006, p 2)

c) Mercer and Dawes (2008) maintain that ground rules for talk reflect the need for social order in classrooms. _____ rules are by no means peculiar to educational settings.

(Allott and Waugh, 2016, p 19)

d) Of course, non-verbal explanations may work better than any words can do: a model of the solar system, for example, or a photograph of a geographical feature, or a demonstration of how to play a musical instrument. However, _____ are usually accompanied by a verbal commentary in order to ensure full understanding, and many things cannot be explained except through language.

(Allott and Waugh, 2016, p 54)

Linking ideas

If the links between ideas are clear and logical, there is often no need to signify them with particular words. In the example below, it is clear that the second sentence explains the reason for the claim in the first sentence.

> Another important element of active listening is non-verbal communication. It is widely held that words form only a minor percentage of communication …

Sometimes, **punctuation** alone can be used to signify a link, as in the example below, where a colon is used to signal that what follows is an expansion and explanation.

> Most skilled teachers take an eclectic approach: they have an awareness of the strengths and weaknesses of the various perspectives and models, and they use their professional judgement to select a pedagogical approach most suitable for a given set of circumstances.

CROSS REFERENCE

Chapter 4, Language in use, Punctuation and sentence structure, Colons

However, often particular words and phrases can be used to signal the relationship between ideas, as in the examples below.

A

Previous qualitative research has looked at teachers who had left the profession. Hale, **for example**, presented powerful narratives of nine teachers' experiences of SATs and the effect these had on their decision to leave the profession.

B

There have been a number of studies investigating teachers' views on the SATs (Jeffrey et al, 1998; Kitchen et al, 1998; Elwiss et al, 1999). **However**, there are limited in-depth explorations of teachers' experiences.

C

Although both aspects are necessary for success, some children will need to be given more support with language comprehension, **while** others will require greater support with word recognition.

D

Primary education in England has, **despite** some outward appearances, changed considerably since the 1970s.

E

English lexicon features many words that can cause confusion **because** they sound like other words but are spelled differently (homophones such as *sew*, *so* and *sow*; *see* and *sea*; *there*, *their* and *they're*).

F

This requires children to understand a concept before they explain it to others but it clearly shows the benefit of retelling **in order to** fully retain what has been learnt.

G

Data were collected on the activities of 25 students on teaching practice placements in primary schools. **In addition**, interviews were carried out over a three-week period.

H

Retelling techniques such as stories through puppets, character studies in costume, events through figures and experiences through pictures would, **therefore**, be of benefit for every class in the primary school.

I

Unfortunately many teachers do not see the value of teaching spelling and its importance is **thus** diminished in children's eyes.

These linking words and phrases have very specific functions, as demonstrated in the texts above:

- **addition**: in addition to, also
- **exemplification**: for example
- **purpose**: in order to
- **contrast**: while, however, despite, though
- **reason**: because
- **result**: thus, therefore
- **condition**: given, if

This means they are not easily interchangeable. They should not be used as decoration or to make a text 'sound more academic'. In fact, they should only be introduced into the text when the relationship between ideas is not already clear enough.

Certain linking words and phrases can act as explicit **signposts** for the reader, letting them know, for example, why something is included in the text, or what is coming next.

A

One aspect of active listening is verbal communication on the part of the listener such as restating and summarising the speaker's message (Jagger, 2015). **Another important element of active listening is** body language.

B

The aim of this essay is to examine the extent to which communication can be considered to be the **core** teaching skill. **It will begin by** examining what is meant by the term 'communication' in teaching. **It will then** outline what are generally considered to be the core skills required by teachers, with reference to the Teachers' Standards (2012). It will go on to examine the impact of communication skills on a range of teaching and learning activities, and the role that poor communication has played in a number of documented 'failures' in education.

The first example illustrates a structure which is useful for sequencing information and linking new information to a central theme. (Repetition is also important here.) The second example contains typical signposts from essay introductions.

There are clearly many ways to link ideas. The important thing is to make choices based on *meaning*, and the needs of the reader.

Task

Linking ideas

1) Choose the word/phrase which conveys the right meaning in the passages below.

   a) Data were collected on the activities of 25 students on teaching practice placements in primary schools. In addition/Moreover, interviews were carried out over a three-week period.

   b) A number of students reported that they had been given insufficient support, particularly in response to difficult situations. In contrast/On the contrary, others praised their school-based tutors for the support they had given them.

   c) Some students were involved in the communities where their placement schools were situated, however/albeit in different social contexts.

   d) Phonics is one of the systems thereby/whereby children learn to read with confidence.

   e) Shared writing exercises in the class give pupils a good model, hereby/ thereby encouraging them to express their own ideas.

   f) The report explored the needs of a subgroup of special needs pupils, namely/ in other words, those with dyslexia and learning difficulties.

   g) It was reported that most children said they enjoyed English and Maths lessons (84% and 81% respectively/namely).

h) There are concerns of a 'two-tier' system comprising teachers who have taken a PGCE qualification and those who have undertaken school-based QTS training, with the first/the former having more status, and the latter/the last being seen as a less professional option.

2) Delete any linking words or phrases which are unnecessary, do not convey the right meaning, or are grammatically incorrect in the following text.

Dyslexia is a common learning difficulty that can cause problems with reading, writing and spelling. Furthermore, it is a 'specific learning difficulty', which means it causes problems with certain abilities used for learning, such as reading and writing. However, it has been estimated that up to one in every ten to twenty people in the UK has some degree of dyslexia. Given that dyslexia is a lifelong problem that can present challenges on a daily basis, but support is available to improve reading and writing skills and help those with the problem be successful at school and work. While signs of dyslexia usually become apparent when a child starts school and begins to focus more on learning how to read and write. However, people with dyslexia often have good skills in other areas, such as creative thinking and problem solving.

Developing a coherent argument and expressing criticality

In order to develop a coherent argument, it is necessary to put yourself in the reader's shoes and imagine what the reader will want to know. You must anticipate their questions and guide them carefully through your argument, providing clear signposts so that they don't get lost or stuck. Imagine a very demanding reader!

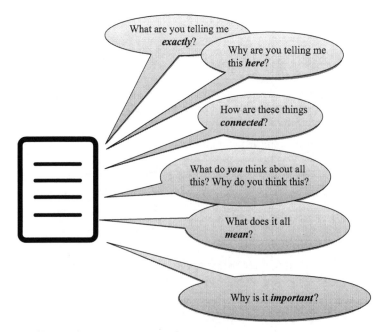

Figure 2.1: Anticipating the reader's questions

Task

Developing a coherent argument

Below is an essay title from a literacy module:

Discuss the role of 'classic' literature in the study of English in schools.

Read the student's discussion of the background to this issue and consider these questions.

1) Do you find the text easy to follow?

2) How has the student made it easy for you? Have they used any of the patterns discussed in this chapter, such as general/specific information, old/new information, referring back in the text, linking and signposts?

3) Have they guided you through their argument and expressed their stance? How?

Many ideas and phrases from what is regarded as 'classic' children's literature, from the nineteenth and early twentieth century, have become deeply embedded in everyday language. The National Curriculum (DfE, 2013) includes a requirement for children in Years 3–4 to 'listen to, discuss and express views about … classic fiction … at a level beyond that at which they can read independently'. Clearly this recognises possibilities for extending imaginative horizons, enriching understanding of other and earlier societies, and developing an understanding of how language use changes over time, all of which form a strong argument for the inclusion of reading such stories as a 'class book'.

Nevertheless, a survey by the British Library (Bloom, 2014) found that children often struggle to engage with the style and the attitudes of these bygone writers, or to think of them as 'real'. Archaic vocabulary or phrasing can cause problems, social attitudes of the time may no longer be acceptable in modern society, and details of life from the book may need long and complicated explanations. Gubar (2009, p vii) has also suggested that many classic texts 'failed to engage with the complexities of contemporary life, and promoted a static and highly idealised picture of childhood as a time of primitive simplicity'.

However, there is a great deal to be said in favour of introducing at an early age texts which reach beyond everyday experience. A pupil who has been introduced to, for instance, Maggie Tulliver or Tom Sawyer in the classroom is perhaps more likely to explore *The Mill on the Floss* or *The Adventures of Tom Sawyer* as an independent reader later. A text such as *The Secret Garden* can open children's awareness of topics from life in great houses, to the contrasting lives of rich and poor in Edwardian times, to gardening and so on. Indeed, to a whole range of historical and philosophical lines of thought! Reading which extends a child's knowledge of and perspective on the world can positively enhance that child's potential and meaningful development as a critical reader.

Discussion: developing a coherent argument

Paragraph 1

This paragraph starts with a statement directly responding to the question, which the writer then supports with a quotation from official documentation. The writer's viewpoint is signalled by the use of positive terms such as 'clearly', 'extending', 'enriching' and 'developing', and the point is emphasised by the reference to 'a strong argument'.

Paragraph 2

The second paragraph starts with the marker, 'Nevertheless', making it clear that the opposite point of view will be presented. Again relevant references and quotations are provided, and the writer uses terms with negative connotations such as 'struggle', 'problems', 'not acceptable' and 'complicated explanations'.

Paragraph 3

The third paragraph begins with a very explicit signpost, 'However', which indicates that the argument is going to be positive. There are then specific examples of texts which might be used, and learning opportunities these might give rise to. There are positive markers making the writer's stance clear, such as 'enhance', 'extend' and 'meaningful development'. There is reference back to the topic of the first paragraph, reinforcing the idea that such texts will include themes outside children's experiences and may be more challenging than the texts they might read independently.

CROSS
REFERENCE

Chapter 1,
Academic
writing: text,
process and
criticality,
Writing
critically

The language of criticality

When constructing an argument, writers need to use specific language to express their criticality and their stance (Biber, 2006; Argent, 2017). This includes how certain you are about something, how strongly you feel about something, and the extent to which you are convinced by evidence and the opinions of others. Some examples of this type of language use were mentioned in the previous task, eg:

- the use of language which explicitly conveys opinion ('clearly', 'there is a great deal to be said in favour of', 'can positively enhance', 'can cause problems', 'indeed');

- the use of **summary noun phrases** which convey interpretation or opinion regarding what has been previously mentioned ('these bygone writers', 'such classic texts');

- the interpretation of supporting literature through the choice of reporting verbs and expressions ('found that', 'has also suggested');

- the use of language which conveys degrees of certainty, including the use of cautious language to avoid overgeneralisation or unsubstantiated claims ('form a strong argument', 'there is a great deal to be said', 'often struggle', 'can cause', 'may need', 'many classic texts', 'can positively enhance').

Task

Identifying stance

Writers have different views depending on the extent of their knowledge and their interpretation of a situation. How do the following sentences differ in the way the writers assess the situation in question?

1a) This approach will limit the negative effects of the diagnosis of a specific learning disability.

1b) This approach may limit the negative effects of the diagnosis of a specific learning disability.

2a) Concerns relating to pupil care have been addressed.

2b) Concerns relating to pupil care have to some extent been addressed.

3a) The reason for the decline in illiteracy is improved education.

3b) The principal reason for the reported decline in illiteracy is improved education.

4a) Schools are currently facing numerous serious problems.

4b) Schools are currently facing a number of challenges.

5a) Further research is required on this innovative approach.

5b) Further research is required on this largely untested approach.

6a) Lawlor argues that changes in funding will impact poorer communities disproportionately.

6b) Wright claims that changes in funding will impact poorer communities disproportionately.

6c) Marosi et al maintain that changes in funding will impact poorer communities disproportionately.

7a) Mason et al advocate the use of calculators.

7b) Rowe suggests the use of calculators.

7c) Houghton discourages the use of calculators.

8a) All the teachers share information.

8b) Crucially, all teachers share information.

8c) Worryingly, all the teachers share information.

Discussion: identifying stance

- In 1), 'will' suggests that the writer has been convinced of the certainty of the 'proposition' (ie the approach does x); 'may' suggests uncertainty on the part of the writer regarding the proposition. The writers are clearly assessing the evidence in different ways.

- In 2), 'to some extent' suggests that the writer believes that many concerns have not yet been addressed.

- In 3), 'principal' suggests that the writer believes there are also other (less important) reasons; the choice of the word 'reported' serves to distance the writer from the claim slightly.

- In 4), 'numerous' means 'many'; 'a number of' means 'some'; the term 'serious problems' suggests a more negative assessment of the situation than 'challenges'.

- In 5), 'innovative' suggests a positive assessment of the situation; 'largely untested' suggests that the writer has concerns.

- In 6), 'argues' suggests that the writer believes Lawlor has presented a convincing, well-supported case; 'claims' suggests that the writer sees Wright's view as open to question; 'maintains' suggests that the writer believes Marosi et al are insisting on a view which goes against the majority view or evidence to the contrary.

- In 7), the writers express their interpretation of scholars' views through the choice of verb: 'advocate' means that they strongly recommend something; 'suggest' implies a much weaker recommendation; 'discourage' conveys the opposite of a recommendation.

- In 8), a) is a neutral report of a situation; the addition of the word 'crucially' suggests the writer's belief that this fact is very important or positive; the addition of 'worryingly' suggests the writer's concern about the situation.

Summary

This chapter has looked at the ways in which you can make your writing clear and coherent. It has demonstrated how careful planning and editing can help you to produce a text which a reader can easily navigate and understand. It has shown how to write effective introductions and conclusions, and how to structure clear paragraphs. It has made clear how your choice of language can affect meaning, and impact on the understanding of the reader. It has also demonstrated how arguments can be developed coherently, and expressed through the use of 'critical' language.

Sources of example texts

Allott, K and Waugh, D (2016) *Language and Communication in Primary Schools*. London: Sage.

Gill, A and Waugh, D (2017) *Phonics: Getting It Right in a Week*. Northwich: Critical Publishing.

McGuinness, D (2006) Some Comments on a Report by Torgerson, C, Brooks, G and Hall, J. [online] Available at: www.rrf.org.uk/Torgersonarticle.pdf (accessed 19 March 2018).

Waugh, D and Neaum, S (eds) (2013) *Beyond Early Reading*. Northwich: Critical Publishing.

References

Argent, S (2017) The Language of Critical Thinking. [online] Available at: www.baleap.org/event/eap-northcritical-thinking (accessed 27 February 2017).

Benson, P and Heidish, P (1995) The ESL Expert: Writing Processes and Classroom Practices. In Belcher, D and Braine, G (eds) *Academic Writing in a Second Language: Essays on Research and Pedagogy.* Norwood, NJ: Ablex, 313–30.

Biber, D (2006) Stance in Spoken and Written University Registers. *Journal of English for Academic Purposes*, 5(2), 97–116.

Drummond, A (2016) An Investigation of Noun Frequencies in Cohesive Nominal Groups. *Journal of Second Language Teaching and Research*, 5(1), 62–88.

Flowerdew, J (2003) Signalling Nouns in Discourse. *English for Specific Purposes*, 22(4), 329–46.

Halliday, M and Hasan, R (1976) *Cohesion in English*. London: Longman.

Jordon, R (2001) *Academic Writing Course: Study Skills in English*. 3rd ed. Harlow, Essex: Pearson Education Limited.

Chapter 3
Referring to sources

This chapter focuses on referencing, one of the most important academic skills you need to acquire if you are to be successful in your studies. It explains why referencing is so important and how you should go about doing it in your own work. It also discusses how to use sources critically, and how to avoid plagiarism, while illustrating how these two things are often interrelated.

Terminology

The term 'referencing' is generally understood to refer to:

- in-text referencing – the occasions in the main body of a text where you refer to, or quote, the work of others (ie your *sources*);
- the list at the end of the text (usually entitled 'References'), where you list all the sources you have referred to, or quoted, in the text.

In-text references are also sometimes referred to as 'citations', and the verbs 'reference' and 'cite' are both used to refer to the practice of referring to sources.

Why should I reference?

Accurate referencing of academic work is essential for the following reasons.

- It is a form of academic 'courtesy', both to the writer (by acknowledging their work) and to the reader (by helping them to find the source easily).

- It indicates that you have consulted authorities and checked your facts, allowing the reader to have confidence in what you write.

- It signals that you have contextualised your ideas in a wider framework, linking your work to work done previously by other scholars.

- It shows the reader that you have used the literature to build your own ideas.

- It signals that your ideas are founded upon scholarship, and thus have credibility.

- It signals you, as a writer, are situated within the educational knowledge community.

- It shows that you are not pretending to be the source of information or ideas found in sources, ie that you are not attempting to **plagiarise**.

How should I reference?

There are two main referencing systems, each named after the universities where they originated:

- The **Harvard** system, sometimes referred to as the 'name-date' or 'author-date' system;
- The **Vancouver** system, sometimes referred to as the 'number' or 'citation-sequence' system.

In education, the Harvard system is used and this will be discussed in detail below.

The Harvard system

In this system, sources are identified in the main body of the text according to the surname(s) of the author(s) and the publication year of the source, usually separated by a comma. At the end of the text, all references mentioned in the text are presented in **alphabetical order**, according to author surname (or the surname of the first author when there are multiple authors). Note that the reference forms part of the clause or sentence, so comes before any punctuation.

Example (main text)

Research demonstrates that when this is implemented properly, cooperative learning presents an ideal method of supporting not only children's learning but also the effective use of talk (Johnson and Johnson, 1989; Slavin, 1995, 1996; Sharan, 1990; Jenkins et al, 2003, Kyndt et al, 2013). The first step is to ensure that pupils are supported to develop the necessary interpersonal and small-group skills to cooperate. The second step is to structure the tasks to maximise the potential to cooperate.

(Jolliffe and Waugh, 2017, p 47)

Example (final reference list)

Jenkins, J, Antil, L, Wayne, S and Vadasy, P (2003) How Cooperative Learning Works for Special Education and Remedial Students. *Exceptional Children*, 69, 279–92.

Johnson, D W and Johnson, R (1989) *Cooperation and Competition: Theory and Research*. Edina, MN: Interaction Book Company.

Kyndt, E, Raes, E, Lismont, B, Timmers, F, Cascallar, E and Dochy, F (2013) A Meta-analysis of the Effects of Face-to-face Cooperative Learning: Do Recent Studies Falsify or Verify Earlier Findings? *Educational Research Review*, 10, 133–49.

Slavin, R E (1995) *Cooperative Learning: Theory, Research, and Practice*. Boston: Allyn and Bacon.

Sharan, S (1990) *Cooperative Learning: Theory and Research*. Westport, CT: Praeger.

CROSS REFERENCE

Studying for your Education Degree, Chapter 3, Becoming a member of your academic and professional community

Referencing styles

Within the Harvard system, there are slight variations between publishers. Each publisher has a particular style – sometimes called a 'house style' – of referencing, ie how they want references presented in their books, journals, etc. This will be a version of the Harvard system, with their own particular specifications regarding, for example, the way names are given or the use of commas. This book uses the Harvard system, and examples of Harvard referencing are given in the house style of the book's publisher, Critical Publishing.

A well-known example of a particular style in education disciplines is APA, the style of the American Psychological Association. Your university and your specific department will almost certainly have their own styles: they may adopt a style such as APA, or they may devise their own style. It is essential to know which style is required in a particular assignment. Once you are sure of the requirements, the important thing is to provide references which are **complete**, **accurate** and **consistent**. Some common style variations will be mentioned in the following sections.

Using the Harvard system

In education, you will probably be required to use the Harvard system. This section provides general guidelines.

In-text conventions in the Harvard system

In terms of in-text usage, the Harvard system is slightly more complicated than the number system, and there are some conventions that you should be aware of.

Multiple references

When listing multiple sources in the main body of text, it is usually the convention to list them chronologically, with publications from the same year listed alphabetically; they are usually separated with semi-colons, eg:

(Li, 2002; James and Roberts, 2007; Jones, 2007)

If an author has published two works in the same year, the year is followed by a, b etc (explained in more detail later in the chapter), eg:

(Li, 2002b)

Direct quotations

Quotations should be used judiciously. Overuse of quotation can be a symptom of an uncritical 'patchwork' use of references, or even plagiarism. You should only quote something if it is particularly interesting or powerful, and it is not always necessary, or most effective, to quote whole sentences (see example below).

CROSS REFERENCE

Using sources critically

In your text:

- Direct quotations are usually enclosed in 'single' or "double" inverted commas. Follow any guidelines provided on this by your lecturers and be consistent throughout the text.

- A full sentence quotation is introduced with a colon; quoted words or phrases are integrated into your own sentences.

- Page numbers must be provided as part of the reference.

- A quotation must be copied *exactly* as it is written in the book or article from which it has been taken.

- Any words missed out must be indicated by the use of an ellipsis (three dots …). (Sometimes these are enclosed in square brackets to indicate that the omission is yours and not the original author's.)

- Any words inserted or changed (to make the quotation fit in with your own grammar and meaning) must be enclosed in square brackets.

- Long quotations require double indenting and/or a smaller typeface.

Examples

Longer quote

According to Richie and Lewis (2003, p 185):

> A good focus group is more than the sum of its parts. The researcher harnesses the group process, encouraging the group to work together to generate more in-depth data based on interaction […]. [He or she] helps the group create a reflective environment in which the group can take an issue, approach it as they choose and explore it fully.

Shorter quotes

Richie and Lewis (2003) see a good focus group as 'more than the sum of its parts' (p 185). The researcher facilitates the group dynamic, leading to the generation of 'more in-depth data based on interaction' (p 185).

The use of 'et al'

The Latin phrase 'et al' means 'and others'. In education, it is not uncommon to find articles written by as many as five or more authors. In such circumstances, in-text referencing can get a bit messy, so the format 'first-author et al' is used whenever there are three or more authors.

Note that in the final reference list, you must list *all* of the authors regardless of how many authors there are, unless a house style demands otherwise.

Compiling your final list of references in the Harvard system

The final reference list appears at the end of an assignment, paper or publication, in alphabetical order in the Harvard system. It is usual to precede the list with the simple heading 'References'. This term implies a **one-to-one match** between in-text references and the sources included in the final reference list, ie if a source is in the reference list, it should have been cited in the main body of text and any citation in the main body of text should be listed in the final reference list. The term 'bibliography' is sometimes used in books; it has the wider sense of 'sources of information on this subject' which generally inform a piece of work; this approach is not suitable in an academic assignment, so the term 'references', with its more restricted meaning, is usually required.

There are essentially three main types of hard copy publication you will come across:

- books;
- chapters in edited books;
- journal articles.

In this section, guidelines will be provided on how to reference these and other types of reference. Examples will follow the house style of Critical Publishing, but remember that styles vary, and you will need to find out what is required in your department.

Referencing books

There are two types of book that you will encounter: **standard textbooks**, where the authors have written the entire textbook from beginning to end, and **edited textbooks**, where many different authors have written individual chapters which are subsequently collated by an editor or group of editors. The general format for referencing textbooks is:

Surname[s] of author[s], Initial[s] (Year) *Title: Subtitle*. Edition [if 2nd or greater]. Place of publication: Publisher.

Examples

Beck, I (2005) *Bringing Words to Life*. New York: Guilford Press.

Crystal, D (2005) *How Language Works*. London: Penguin.

Jolliffe, W and Waugh, D with Carss, A (2015) *Teaching Systematic Synthetic Phonics in Primary Schools*. 2nd ed. London: Learning Matters/SAGE.

When referring to an edited textbook in its entirety, the abbreviation 'ed' (editor) or 'eds' (editors) is inserted before the publication year.

Examples

Brock, C (ed) (2015) *Education in the United Kingdom*. London: Bloomsbury.

Jones, D and Hodson, P (eds) (2017) *Unlocking Speaking and Listening: Developing Spoken Language in the Primary Classroom*. 3rd ed. London: David Fulton.

Waugh, D and Neaum, S (eds) (2013) *Beyond Early Reading*. London: Critical Publishing.

Referencing chapters in edited books

It is important to distinguish between a straightforward textbook and an edited textbook when referencing. With edited books, different people write the individual chapters and each chapter is treated as a separate article. This means that if students read and make reference to, say, four chapters in an edited book with ten chapters, four references will need to be added to the reference list. The general format for chapters in edited textbooks is:

Surname[s] of chapter author[s], Initial[s] (Year) Title of Chapter. In Surname[s] of editor[s] of book, Initial[s] (ed[s]) *Title of Book: Subtitle of Book*. Edition [if 2nd or greater]. Place of publication: Publisher.

Examples

English, E (2017) Is There a Place for Drama? In Waugh, D, Jolliffe, W and Allott, K (eds) *Primary English for Trainee Teachers*. London: Sage.

English, E (2015) Writing and Drama. In Waugh, D, Neaum, S and Bushnell, A (eds) *Beyond Early Writing*. Northwich: Critical Publishing.

Referencing journal articles

The general format for journal articles is:

Surname[s] of author[s], Initial[s] (Year) Title of Article. *Journal Title*, Volume(Part), Pages.

Examples

Apthorp, H (2006) Effects of a Supplemental Vocabulary Programme in Third Grade Reading/Language Arts. *Journal of Educational Research*, 100(2), 67–79.

Shapiro, L and Solity, J (2008) Delivering Phonological and Phonics Training within Whole-Class Teaching. *British Journal of Educational Psychology*, 78, 597–620.

Solity, J and Vousden, J (2009) Real Books vs Reading Schemes: A New Perspective from Instructional Psychology. *Educational Psychology*, 29(4), 469–511.

Since PDF copies of journal articles are identical to their print counterparts, it is acceptable to reference electronically accessed versions as the print counterpart, since this will provide sufficient information for a reader (or marker) to locate the resource if required.

In addition, the use of the 'digital object identifier' (DOI) – which is a permanent address for documents on the internet – is likely to become more prevalent in the future. Thus, all of the following variants for referencing journal articles are acceptable in student work:

Friars, P and Mellor, D (2009) Drop-Out from Parenting Training Programmes: A Retrospective Study. *Journal of Child and Adolescent Mental Health*, 21(1), 29–38.

Friars, P and Mellor, D (2009) Drop-Out from Parenting Training Programmes: A Retrospective Study. *Journal of Child and Adolescent Mental Health*, 21(1), 29–38. Available at: www.tandfonline.com/doi/pdf/10.2989/JCAMH.2009.21.1.5.807 (accessed 7 January 2015).

Friars, P and Mellor, D (2009) Drop-Out from Parenting Training Programmes: A Retrospective Study. *Journal of Child and Adolescent Mental Health*, 21(1), 29–38. DOI:10.2989/JCAMH.2009.21.1.5.807

Theses and dissertations

Theses and dissertations (for example, PhD and MSc theses) follow a format that is very similar to books, except following the title, [type of thesis], [location of university: name of university] appears, for example:

Clark, D (1985) *Small Schools: What Are the Factors Affecting Small Schools' Co-operation?* Unpublished M.Ed. dissertation. Exeter: University of Exeter School of Education.

Waugh, D (2000) *Primary Schools at the Crossroads: A Study of Primary Schools' Abilities to Implement Educational Change, with a Particular Focus on Small Primary Schools.* Unpublished PhD thesis. Hull: University of Hull.

Conference proceedings

Conference proceedings are printed documents reflecting the content of a conference. They are dealt with in the same way as chapters in edited textbooks.

Example

Keast, D (1993) *Exeter Small Schools' Network Newsletter Spring 1993 and Conference Digest.* Exeter: Exeter Small Schools' Network, University of Exeter.

Newspapers and magazines

Occasionally, you might need to reference an article in a newspaper or magazine, but bear in mind the quality of the newspaper or magazine being used. The format for newspapers and magazines is much the same as for journal articles, except that the full date of the issue is required.

Example

Marks, N (2014) Guardian Readers Reveal What Makes Them Happy at Work. *The Guardian*, 11 June. [online] Available at: www.theguardian.com/sustainable-business/happy-work-what-makes-you (accessed 25 October 2016).

Organisational or 'corporate' authors

Institutions and organisations produce many papers and documents. These often cause referencing problems. Remember, however, that these institutions and organisations can be authors in their own right and thus it is fairly easy to reference material by these bodies as the name you need for a name-year system is simply the organisation's name.

So the Department for Education, the National Literacy Trust and Ofsted can all be cited as authors – DfE (2011), National Literacy Trust (2014) and Ofsted (2010), for example.

Examples

DfE (2011) *Teachers' Standards: Statutory Guidance for School Leaders, School Staff and Governing Bodies*. London: DFE-00066-2011.

National Literacy Trust (2014) *Children and Young People's Reading in 2014*. London: National Literacy Trust.

Ofsted (2010) *The Annual Report of Her Majesty's Chief Inspector 2009/10*. Norwich: The Stationery Office.

Common problems in referencing

'Anonymous' authors

With some documents, such as dictionaries or Acts of Parliament, it is difficult to find out who the author is. In these cases, it is acceptable to reference by the document or series title.

Examples

Collins English Dictionary (2011) 11th ed. Glasgow: William Collins & Sons.

Education Reform Act (1988) London: HMSO.

Authors with multiple outputs in the same year

Some authors produce several publications in one year. If two or more articles are attributed to the same author or group of authors in a particular year, you need to use some means of distinguishing between the articles. For example, if you use three papers written by Dianne Jones and published in 2004 in an assignment, how would a reader know which paper 'Jones (2004)' refers to? It could be any of the three. (This isn't a problem with Vancouver-style approaches as you would give each paper a separate number as you used it.)

The way to do this in the Harvard system is to use alphabetical sequencing (a, b, c, etc) to distinguish between the articles. So you call the first paper you use Jones (2004a), the second, Jones (2004b), the third, Jones (2004c). The references in the final list would therefore be:

Jones, D (2004a) [Title, etc of first Jones paper you cite.]

Jones, D (2004b) [Title, etc of second Jones paper you cite.]

Jones, D (2004c) [Title, etc of third Jones paper you cite.]

Note that *you*, as the writer, have inserted the letters a, b, c after the publication year. They are not fixed like the publication year, but serve only to distinguish between the three 2004 Jones articles you are using. If you only used one of the Jones papers, you would not need to use any letters after the publication year.

Secondary citations

CROSS REFERENCE

Academic malpractice

Sometimes, students make use of references they find in books and articles they have been reading, but do not actually consult the original sources. To present these secondary references as primary references is really a form of academic malpractice. To avoid this, you should ideally follow up the secondary references and consult the original sources. Where this is genuinely not possible, you can make use of the phrases 'cited in' or 'cited by' to acknowledge that the reference is a secondary reference. Secondary references are usually presented as follows:

In the text

(Nash, 1978, cited in Galton and Patrick, 1990, p 9)

In the list of references

Galton, M and Patrick, H (eds) (1990) *Curriculum Provision in the Small Primary School*. London: Routledge.

Electronic sources of information

Increasingly, students are making use of electronic sources of information such as the Internet, e-journals and PDF documents when undertaking assignments. Providing that the information employed is in a legitimate format and from a legitimate source (eg a reputable organisation), such information can be extremely valuable. For in-text referencing, the format for electronic sources of information is very much the same as for hard copy material, ie you need a name and a publication year. For compiling the final reference list, the format for referencing electronic material is similar to the format for books and journal articles, except that some additional information is required:

- The type of medium – webpage, PDF, DVD, computer program, etc. – is required (in square brackets) after the resource/document details.

- Following the type of medium, use the phrase 'Available at' or 'Available from' followed by information about the source of the material used, eg the specific computer program, web page, etc.
- The access date (in brackets) is required after the source.
- If no creation/publication date is available for the electronic material, simply write 'no date' where the publication year would normally go.
- If no author can be found, follow the guidance given above for anonymous authors.

Examples

Merriam-Webster Dictionary. [online] Available at: www.merriam-webster.com (accessed 15 May 2017).

Wall, K, Hall, E, Baumfield, V, Higgins, S, Rafferty, V, Remedios, R, Thomas, U, Tiplady, L, Towler, C and Woolner, P (2010) *Learning to Learn in Schools and Learning to Learn in Further Education.* Campaign for Learning. [online] Available at: www.campaign-for-learning.org.uk (accessed 17 October 2016).

There is still debate about how to reference electronic material correctly so don't worry too much about any minor differences in approaches that you come across.

Variations in referencing

Although referencing systems are dependent on some set rules, there is a degree of flexibility, mainly brought about by differences in the house styles of various publishers and organisations. The important thing is to follow guidelines and to make sure that your references are complete, accurate and consistent – don't mix and match in the same piece of work. The following variations are common in the Harvard system:

In-text

- A comma is usual between the name and date, but is sometimes omitted, eg (Thomas 2016) rather than (Thomas, 2016).
- Page numbers for direct quotes can be either preceded by a comma and 'p' or 'p.' ('pp' or 'pp.' for a page range), or by a colon, eg (Thomas, 2016, p. 36) or (Thomas, 2016: 36).
- The phrase 'et al' is sometimes written 'et al.' or '*et al.*'.

Final list

- For journal articles, **bold** is often used to indicate volumes, eg:
  Weisberg, D S, Keil, F C, Goodstein, J, Rawson, E and Gray, J R (2008) The Seductive Allure of Neuroscience Explanations. *Journal of Cognitive Neuroscience*, **20**(3), 470–477.
- Page numbers are sometimes preceded by p/pp or p./pp.
- Initials are often followed with full stops to indicate the abbreviation, eg:
  Geake, J. (2008) Neuromyths in Education. *Educational Research*, 50(2), 123–133.
- Full first names are sometimes used instead of initials, eg:
  Bruner, Jerome (1986) *Actual Minds, Possible Worlds.* Cambridge, MA: Harvard University Press.

- The abbreviations 'ed' and 'eds' are often followed by full stops – 'ed.', 'eds.'
- Titles can be in lower case (apart from the first word and proper nouns), or they can be capitalised throughout (apart from 'grammar' words such as prepositions and pronouns), or they can distinguish between titles and subtitles, eg:

Swales, J and Feak, C (2012) *Academic writing for graduate students: essential tasks and skills*. 3rd ed. Michigan: Michigan ELT.

Swales, J and Feak, C (2012) *Academic Writing for Graduate Students: Essential Tasks and Skills*. 3rd ed. Michigan: Michigan ELT.

Swales, J and Feak, C (2012) *Academic Writing for Graduate Students: Essential tasks and skills*. 3rd ed. Michigan: Michigan ELT.

Task

Referencing errors

1) Below are a number of entries than might appear in a text. What problems can you identify and correct?

   a) According to Jolliffe and Waugh, four modes of language interrelate to produce literacy.

   b) The major hindrance appears to be the cultural dominance of 'technical rationality'. Schön 1988.

   c) In a theoretical paper, Dickoff and James (1968) argue this position, which is subsequently backed up by a further, data-based paper (Dickoff and James 1968).

   d) Meleis [2001] speculates that historical and cultural paternalism are largely to blame.

   e) To quote from Johnston and Watson 2007: Learners acquire phoneme awareness better in the context of letters and print compared to learning without this concrete support.

   f) According to Gill, A and Waugh, D (2017) teachers use many activities to attune learners to sounds all around them.

   g) The results are consistent with the findings of Posner, Wilson and Kraj (2012).

   h) Smith [cited by Jones 2014] suggests that the findings are incomplete.

   i) … (see, for example, Lewin's 'change spiral' in his book of 1958).

   j) (Schön 1988) suggests that this paradox can be resolved by acknowledging the importance of subjectivity.

2) Below are entries that might appear in a final reference list. What problems can you identify and correct?

   a) David Crystal (2005) HOW LANGUAGE WORKS. London: Penguin.

   b) DCSF *Teaching effective vocabulary: What can teachers do to increase the vocabulary of children who start education with a limited vocabulary?* Nottingham: DCSF. 2008.

   c) DfE (2013) The national curriculum in England: Key stages 1 and 2 framework document.

   d) H. Dombey, (2009) ITE English: Readings for Discussion December 2009 www.ite.org.uk/ite_readings/simple_view_reading.pdf

e) Ings, R (2009) Writing is Primary. Action research on the teaching of writing in primary schools. www.nawe.co.uk/Private/17646/Live/Writing-is-Primary.pdf

f) Meek (2010) *Readings about reading.* Changing English: Studies in Culture and Education, 11(2): 307–17.

g) *Teaching Children to Read: an evidence-based assessment of the scientific research literature on reading and its implications for reading instruction. Reports of subgroups.* NICHD. National Reading Panel (2000).

h) Rooke, J. (2013) www.literacytrust.org.uk/assets/0001/9256/Transforming_Writing_Final_Report.pdf (accessed 17 January 2018).

Top tips

Referencing software

There are a number of referencing software packages that you may choose to use, eg **Endnote**, **Mendeley**, **Zotero** and **Papyrus**, but this is a purely personal decision. They have advantages: they ensure that there is always a one-to-one match between your in-text references and those listed in the final reference list; you can switch automatically and painlessly between different house styles (even between Harvard and Vancouver). They also have disadvantages: you may not be able to get the software on your home computer without buying it (and it can be quite expensive); their integration into word processing packages can be problematic, causing formatting glitches, for example.

Using sources critically

It is important to know the rules for referencing, but this is just part of the bigger picture. Many students feel confused about referencing. Look at the typical comments below. Do you ever feel like this?

Case studies

1) 'I worry about using too many references. I think it won't be my ideas in the essay.'

2) 'I found a lot of good quotes for my essay, but the lecturer said it was too descriptive and that I didn't have an argument.'

3) 'I spent ages paraphrasing – changing every word of the original text so that I don't plagiarise and get into trouble. But the lecturer didn't think I had understood the ideas in the literature. She also said my language was "awkward".'

4) 'I found lots of opinions on this subject but I don't know how to make them into an essay.'

5) 'The lecturer said I should give my own opinion, but I'm worried that I'm not as expert as the people writing in books and journals.'

These concerns are understandable. Using sources critically is one of the biggest challenges of university study, and well-meaning advice can often appear contradictory. Firstly, it is important to understand that using references is not a negative thing. On the contrary, it is a positive thing, as it shows you have researched the topic. However, in order for references to enhance your work, they must be used *critically*. Table 3.1 illustrates exactly what this means.

Table 3.1: Critical use of sources

UNCRITICAL USE OF SOURCES	CRITICAL USE OF SOURCES
Other voices dominate your essay.	References to other scholars support your voice, but don't replace it.
You mostly *describe* the contents of the literature; you mostly engage in 'knowledge-*telling*' (Bereiter and Scardamalia, 1987).	You describe, *analyse* and *evaluate* the contents of the literature; you engage in 'knowledge-*transforming*', ie *doing* something purposeful with knowledge (Bereiter and Scardamalia, 1987).
You use paraphrase to report what scholars say, staying quite close to the original text and replacing individual words with synonyms (to avoid plagiarism).	You demonstrate understanding by paraphrasing in your own words. You try to convey the sense of the sources you refer to, or to interpret them, in a way that supports your argument and acts as a springboard for your own ideas.
There is an over-reliance on quotation. You build your essay around impressive quotations which you think speak for themselves.	You *explain* quotations and integrate them into your own argument; you use quotations to build, support and underline arguments.
You provide a 'patchwork' of references, merely reporting what each individual says, without considering how sources relate to each other or to your argument.	Sources are grouped according to common threads, or compared and contrasted.
You present sources in a random order.	You identify developments, patterns and relationships in the literature, and this determines their place in your essay.
You expect the reader to make the connection between the literature and the context of the assignment.	You explicitly relate what you find in the literature to the context of the assignment; you establish a clear link between your work and the work previously done by other scholars, showing how it has helped you build your ideas.

Advanced skills

Originality

The concept of originality is often misunderstood. It does not mean that you spontaneously make up your own theory or come up with a brand new idea. It means treating the topic in question in a way that is *unique to you*, perhaps finding a new way of looking at something. This usually entails appraising viewpoints and evidence on a specific topic or issue, and coming up with your own ideas about it based on what you have been convinced by. To be credible, academic work should be grounded in the literature of your discipline, as knowledge can only really advance – in your mind or in the discipline as a whole – if it is based on and builds on what has gone before. So the work and ideas of other scholars should of course feature heavily in your work. However, the strongest voice in your work should always be your own. If you can approach what you read and hear critically, and use the ideas of others not only to explore an area of knowledge, but also to inform and shape your own argument, you will be making an original contribution to the subject.

Task

Critical use of sources

Which texts best demonstrate critical use of sources? How?

A

Coppinger et al (2005) state that literacy problems in the general population frequently commence pre-school. School-based services for early identification and intervention and for literacy difficulties are advocated in the USA (Jones, 2004) and many other European countries (White et al, 2009).

B

As literacy problems in the general population frequently commence pre-school (Coppinger et al, 2005), there is a strong case for embedding the skills of recognition and basic management into wider health and education services. Indeed, school-based services for early identification and intervention and for literacy difficulties in primary schools are advocated in the USA (Jones, 2004) and in many other European countries (White et al, 2009).

C

There have been a number of studies investigating teachers' views on the SATs (Jeffrey et al, 1998; Kitchen et al, 1998; Elwiss et al, 1999). However, there are limited in-depth explorations of teachers' experiences. Existing literature tends to focus on issues such as stress for pupils (Sheffield and Nicholson, 2003), time devoted to revision (McIndoe et al, 2004) and test anxiety (Stock et al, 2004). Previous qualitative research has looked at teachers who had left the profession. Hale, for example, presented powerful narratives of nine teachers' experiences of SATs and the effect these had on their decision to leave the profession.

69

D

There have been a number of studies investigating teachers' views on the SATs (Jeffrey et al, 1998; Kitchen et al, 1998; Elwiss et al, 1999). Sheffield and Nicholson (2003) focus on mothering. McIndoe et al (2004) focus on time devoted to revision. Nancy et al (2004) look at test anxiety. Hale presents powerful narratives of nine teachers' experiences of SATs and the effect these had on their decision to leave the profession.

E

Marquis (2007) questions the effectiveness of intervention strategies for young people with attention deficit hyperactive disorder (ADHD), such as family therapy, and claims that drugs have better outcomes. Butler (2007) believes that most childhood ADHD is self-limiting and does not require extensive intervention. He questions the effectiveness of drugs, claiming that scientific accuracy is being sacrificed to marketing spin, and that there may be a link between taking such drugs in childhood and problems in later life.

F

There is some debate regarding the use of drugs to treat young people. On the one hand, Marquis (2007) points to evidence showing the benefits of treatment with drugs. He suggests that these treatments are more effective than intervention strategies for young people with attention deficit hyperactive disorder (ADHD) such as family therapy. In contrast, Butler (2007) questions the effectiveness of drugs, claiming that scientific accuracy is being sacrificed to marketing spin, and even going so far as to suggest a link between taking drugs and problems in later life. In fact, he questions whether intervention is always necessary, believing that most childhood ADHD is by nature self-limiting.

Discussion: critical use of sources

Texts A, D and E simply repeat what the literature says – the writer's voice is not apparent; text B uses the literature to support an argument ('As ... there is a strong case for ... Indeed ...'). Text C identifies common threads ('limited in-depth explorations of'; 'Existing literature tends to focus on'; 'Previous qualitative research has looked at') and contrasts ('existing' v 'previous'). Text F identifies a clear contrast ('on the one hand', 'in contrast'), and the writer's voice is clearly driving the text ('There is some debate', 'even going so far as', 'in fact').

One simple aspect of criticality in source use is the focus that the writer affords information. One of the ways this expresses itself is in the use of **author-prominent** or **information-prominent** sentences. When writers use author-prominent sentences, they place some degree of importance on *who* has written something, as well as what they have written, and the author's name forms part of the sentence structure, eg:

In contrast, Butler (2007) questions the effectiveness of drugs

When writers use an information-prominent sentence, they focus primarily on *what* is being said, and the author's name is only mentioned in the reference, eg:

(Blair et al, 2005)

In texts B and C, there is a clear focus on information, reflected in the information-prominent sentences. In F (and even E), there is a focus on key players in an important debate. Texts A and D use a mixture of information- and author-focused sentences, but their use appears to be quite random.

Task

Focus

1) Identify which of the sentences below are:

- author-prominent;
- information prominent.

2) In author prominent sentences, a writer can convey their view of a scholar's ideas with the verbs or expressions they choose to use to report them. Which verbs and expressions are used in the author-prominent examples?

a) As Wright (1993) points out, one of the paradoxes of successful change is that it escapes public notice simply because it is successful.

b) One of the paradoxes of successful change is that it escapes public notice simply because it is successful (Wright, 1993).

c) According to Oster (2011), cooperative learning has been used to develop a wide range of purposeful learning for primary-aged pupils.

d) Cooperative learning has been used to develop a wide range of purposeful learning for primary-aged pupils (Oster, 2011).

e) Warrington et al (2013) argue that teaching will only really develop as a profession if teachers become more political.

f) Teaching will only really develop as a profession if teachers become more political (Warrington et al, 2013).

3) Listed below are some verbs commonly used by writers to convey their understanding and interpretation of the literature.

acknowledge; advocate; argue that; identify; define something as; distinguish between

Below are some education texts, followed by a student's paraphrase. Choose the best verb from the list above to complete each paraphrase so that it conveys the sense of the original text.

A

Text

Teaching assistants are crucial in improving the experience of children with specific learning difficulties and to do this they need to be appropriately trained in the identification of specific learning difficulties.

(Whiteman et al, 2016, p 31)

Paraphrase

Whiteman et al (2016) _____ targeted training for teaching assistants.

B

Text

Following data analysis, four principal themes emerged from the data, each containing several subthemes.

(Barwick et al, 2011, p 82)

Paraphrase

Barwick et al (2011) _____ four principal themes.

C

Text

Like most qualitative findings, elements may only be transferrable to similar contexts.

(Lingen-Stallard et al, 2016, p 37)

Paraphrase

Lingen-Stallard et al (2016) _____ the limitations of the study.

D

Text

Dyslexia may be mild or severe. While children with milder forms might be supported by a class teacher, more severe forms will need specialist input from people with specific expertise.

(Broadbent, 2015, p 7)

Paraphrase

Broadbent (2015) _____ mild and severe forms of dyslexia.

E

Text

One of the most original thinkers about primary and secondary education, who was, in many ways, years ahead of his time, was Sir Alec Clegg.

(Waugh, 2015, p 18)

Paraphrase

Waugh (2015) _____ Sir Alec Clegg was a pioneer in primary and secondary education.

F

Text

Behaviour problems often arise when children are bored or under-occupied in the classroom.

(Dodd, 2018, p 6)

Paraphrase

Dodd _____ 'behaviour problems are linked to children being bored or under-occupied' (2015, p 6).

Academic malpractice

Academic malpractice includes any practice whereby a student attempts to gain credit that they do not deserve. Academic malpractice is a disciplinary offence in almost all universities and it can have severe consequences. The most common types of academic malpractice are:

- **plagiarism** – using the ideas, work or words of others without clear acknowledgement;
- **collusion** – hiding the contribution of others in your work;
- **falsification** – or fabrication of results.

Most written assignments are screened using software such as **Turnitin**. Turnitin alerts lecturers to possible instances of plagiarism or collusion. Work that shows a significant match with the literature or with an essay by another student will be closely scrutinised by assessors. Serious and/or repeated incidences of plagiarism/collusion will be penalised (a mark of zero is typical, sometimes without an option to resubmit) and may also lead to a disciplinary hearing.

Avoiding academic malpractice is especially important in those studying for a professional qualification, as the Teachers' Standards insist on a person's integrity if they are to enter, or remain on, the appropriate professional register. To achieve qualified teacher status (QTS) 'a teacher is expected to demonstrate consistently high standards of personal and professional conduct', and intentional academic malpractice is likely to be seen as an impediment to good character.

Just as if you were a qualified teacher, charges of malpractice while a student are likely to lead to you being hauled before a disciplinary committee and you could be expelled from the university – and your professional course – if found guilty. These committees are very formal and tend to include the presence of very senior members of the university, and even lawyers.

Top tips

Avoiding plagiarism

Plagiarism can be a result of someone's clear intention to cheat, but often it can arise from a misunderstanding of academic culture and referencing conventions. Always remember the following.

- Acknowledge the sources of *all* information and ideas, whether directly quoted or paraphrased. References are a good thing: they show you have researched the topic, and, used well, they don't detract from your ideas or originality, they enhance them.

- Overuse of quotation can be seen as a type of plagiarism, and it is certainly a symptom of uncritical use of sources. Only quote something if it is particularly interesting or powerful. Think about using effective words and phrases, integrated into your own words, rather than a whole sentence.

- The more you explain and interpret the literature, and the more you integrate it into your own argument and use it to suit your own writing purpose, the less likely you are to plagiarise. Plagiarism is more likely to occur with a 'patchwork' presentation of sources.

Summary

This chapter has explained why and how you should reference. It has outlined the main features of the Harvard system of referencing, and highlighted some common problems encountered by students. It has guided you towards using sources in a critical way to enhance your own writing, and it has examined the issue of academic malpractice and suggested strategies which can help you to avoid it.

Sources of example texts

Jolliffe, W and Waugh, D (eds) (2017) *NQT: The Beginning Teacher's Guide to Outstanding Practice*. London: Sage.

References

Bereiter, C and Scardamalia, M (1987) *The Psychology of Written Composition*. Hillsdale, NJ: Lawrence Erlbaum.

Chapter 4
Language in use

Learning outcomes

After reading this chapter you will:

- have gained knowledge of academic style;

- have developed strategies for improving the clarity of your writing;

- be able to distinguish between formal and informal language with confidence;

- have gained knowledge of useful grammar and punctuation rules and patterns in academic writing;

- be able to avoid some common errors in academic writing.

This chapter provides information and strategies to help develop your control of language for the purpose of academic writing. It will help you to write clearly, and to produce writing which is accurate and academic in style.

Reflection

1) What do you understand by 'academic style'?
2) What challenges do you face when you try to write in an academic style?
3) Are there any aspects of grammar, spelling and punctuation that you struggle with?
4) What resources do you use to help you with writing?

Academic style

You will hear a lot about 'academic style' and 'academic writing' at university. It can sometimes feel as if you are expected to learn a new language, or a different version of the English you know. This can be intimidating, especially if you do not have a lot of recent experience in writing academic essays, or if English is not your first language. Of course, it is necessary to adopt an appropriate style at university, particularly in writing, but there is nothing mysterious about this style. In fact, it could be said to have just three basic characteristics:

- it is clear and easy to read;

- it is concise and precise;

- it is formal in expression.

Clarity

CROSS
REFERENCE

Chapter 2,
Coherent texts
and arguments

The information, ideas and arguments you are required to present in academic essays may be very complex. It is therefore particularly important that the language you use to communicate these things is as clear and readable as possible. As mentioned above, many factors contribute to clarity, some of which will be discussed in this section, some of which are covered in other parts of this book. Clarity and coherence, in particular, are inextricably linked, so you will find many cross references to Chapter 2.

Task

Clarity

Read the two paragraphs below and decide which is clearer and easier to read.

A

There was some research on school size in the period before 1988 which provided a range of different conclusions which did not always agree with each other, and small schools were criticised by some academics and researchers because they were supposed to have narrow curricula and praised and lauded by some academics and researchers who proposed the argument that schools of all sizes had more or less the same curricula before the 1988 Act. Patrick and Hargreaves (1990), for example, looked at small schools and large schools and their curricula and came to the conclusion that the similarities between small schools and large schools were much greater than the differences between small schools and large schools. They summed up their research into the differences between small and large schools and said, 'In answer to the question "Are small schools different?" we have to conclude that, in general, they are not' (1990, p 109).

B

Pre-1988 research on school size provides different and often conflicting conclusions. Criticisms of small schools, based upon a supposed narrowness of the curriculum, have been countered by research which suggests that the curricula of schools of all sizes were broadly the same before the 1988 Act. Patrick and Hargreaves (1990), for example, found that the similarities between small and large schools were much greater than the differences, asserting: 'In answer to the question "Are small schools different?" we have to conclude that, in general, they are not' (1990, p 109).

Discussion: clarity

Text B is taken (in a slightly adapted form) from a doctoral thesis. You probably found it easier to read than Text A. There are a number of reasons for this.

- Text A uses long sentences with separate points connected by 'and'. This often means that the reader has to go back to the beginning, or reread a sentence, to follow the point. Text B is clearer because it uses shorter sentences.

- Text A uses repetition too much; for instance, the phrases 'small schools and large schools' could have been replaced at least once by the pronoun 'them'.

- Text A repeats phrases unnecessarily, eg 'some academics' and 'small and large schools'. Text B is concise. It does not include unnecessary words or phrases.

- Text B uses more concise phrasing; for instance, 'they summed up ... and said' is replaced by 'asserting'.

- Overall, Text B **flows**, whereas Text A is meandering and disjointed, and the reader has to work hard to extract any sense from it. Text B is kinder to the reader: it moves from a general statement in the first sentence to specific details.

Strategies for achieving clarity

From the previous discussion of the two texts, it is clear that there are certain strategies that you can adopt to help you produce clearer writing.

1) Order ideas and sentences in a logical, step-by-step manner, moving from **general to specific** information and ideas.

2) Consider if it will help the reader if you **link back** to the previous sentence before introducing new information, possibly using 'this/these'.

3) Use sensible **repetition** to remind the reader of what is being discussed. This can be seen as a kind of 'lucid repetition' because of how it may facilitate the brain's ability to process information (McIntyre, 1997); note that this is quite different from redundancy, where words or information are repeated for no good reason, often because the text is insufficiently controlled.

4) Do not be afraid of using **short sentences** and **simple language** where these help you communicate difficult ideas clearly. Most academic writing contains a mixture of short and long sentences, but it is important that long sentences are carefully constructed, and that they are not just chains of phrases linked by 'and' or 'but'.

5) Be **concise**. Avoid redundancy and wordiness – throwing down words on the page for their own sake does not make something more academic! Also, remember that you will be required to meet strict word counts in your essays.

6) Be **precise**. Choose words and expressions very carefully so that they convey the exact message you intend. Check that your expression is not vague or ambiguous.

CROSS REFERENCE

Chapter 2, Coherent texts and arguments, General and specific information

CROSS REFERENCE

Chapter 2, Coherent texts and arguments, Old and new information

CROSS REFERENCE

Chapter 2, Coherent texts and arguments, Referring back in the text: repetition, variation and pronoun use

Task

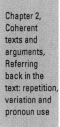

Being concise

Cross out any unnecessary words (ie words which are redundant or which do not add meaning) in the text below.

Roald Dahl was born in the country of Wales, but his parents came from the country of Norway. Roald Dahl was a member of the Royal Air Force in the Second World War, which took place between the years of 1939 and 1945. In the 1940s, Roald Dahl began to become well known for writing stories for both children and adults, and he eventually became one of the best-selling writers of stories in the whole wide world. Roald Dahl's books for children are often very comical and funny and humorous, as well as being quite scary and frightening. Roald Dahl's books for children are many and numerous and they include books such as *The Witches, The Magic Finger, Fantastic Mr Fox, James and the Giant Peach, Charlie and the Chocolate Factory, Matilda, The BFG, The Twits*, as well as others like *George's Marvellous Medicine*. His stories for adults and grown-ups include books like *Tales of the Unexpected* and *Kiss Kiss*.

Task

Being precise

Choose the word or phrase which conveys the most precise meaning in the sentences below.

1) Over the course of the last century, teaching <u>grew/evolved</u> into a highly skilled profession.

2) It is important that trainee teachers show <u>committal/commitment</u> to the profession.

3) The study surveyed teachers to <u>determine/decide</u> their reasons for entering the profession.

4) Children <u>having/exhibiting</u> indicators of dyslexia were not always provided with support.

5) Teachers <u>administer/give</u> standardised tests in Year 6.

6) The study reports on a simple <u>diagnosis/diagnostic</u> test for dyslexia.

7) Improved classroom management has a high impact <u>for/in terms</u> of parent satisfaction.

8) The report details the benefits <u>of/associated with</u> the intervention.

Top tips

Being precise

Avoid using 'etc' or 'and so on'. Also avoid ending sentences with ellipsis (...). Instead use 'such as', 'for example/for instance' with two or three concrete examples.

The study looks into the factors affecting disruptive behaviour – excessive sugar intake, boredom etc.

→ The study looks into the factors affecting disruptive behaviour such as excessive sugar intake and boredom.

Formality

Everybody changes their language to suit the situation they are in: they speak politely and carefully in a job interview; they use relaxed – or sometimes colourful – language among friends; the tone of their emails varies, depending on the recipient.

Task

Identifying formal style

Look at the texts below and decide if they are formal or informal. What is the purpose of each text? Who do you think is the target reader?

A

A lack of positive male role models demonstrating reading as a worthwhile activity has consistently been credited with contributing to the underachievement of boys in reading (Millard, 1996; APPLGC/NLT, 2012). A logical step may be to attempt to increase the number of male teachers in primary schools, so boys would benefit from male reading role models, and motivation and attainment would thus be improved. An extensive, quantitative study conducted by Carrington, Tymms and Merrell (2008) argued that this is not necessarily the case, they 'found no empirical evidence to support the claim there is a tendency for male teachers to enhance the educational performance of boys and, conversely, for female teachers to enhance the educational performance of girls' (p 321). They do, however, also warn against generalisation, and state: 'conceivably, male teachers could have greater salience as role models for boys in the lower primary school, where men are generally conspicuous by their absence … a comparative, possibly longitudinal, investigation of this type is long overdue' (pp 322–3). The discrepancy between boys and girls in reading performance is generally agreed to emerge during KS1, before intensifying with age (Moss, 2000), so perhaps a study of this nature could shed further light on the subject. The Boys' Reading Commission noted 'that the issue is not about female teachers per se, but the lack of male staff in primary schools to model positive reading behaviour and attitudes. This can mean reading is perceived as a female pastime' (APPLGC/NLT, 2012, p 12).

B

Get dad reading

'The best role models seem to be dads, sports coaches and athletes, men the boys aspire to be. If they experience these men reading and sharing their love of books (any kind of books) then reading is not seen as a female occupation.

'Boys in general thrive on competition, action and bursts of intense activity, so the way they are expected to read needs to reflect this. Actors also make good role models – bringing one in to share his thoughts on a play or a screenplay would be cool too.

'Dads and lads sessions work where physical activity is balanced with shared experiences of books and reading can also work. They involve campfire cooking and opportunities to chill out, away from technology, with a good book.'

(Cally Smart, quoted in Marsh, 2015)

C

PA refreshed commitment in schools to promoting reading for enjoyment will strongly benefit boys, who want to read around their interests. To enable this to happen reading for pleasure needs to be an integral element in a school's teaching and learning strategy and teachers need to be supported in their knowledge of relevant quality texts that will engage all pupils. There is a specific danger that a predominantly female workforce will unconsciously privilege texts that are more attractive to girls.

(National Literacy Trust, 2012)

Discussion: identifying formal style

Text A is taken from an academic essay. Text B is taken from an online newspaper. Text C is from 'The Report of the All-Party Parliamentary Literacy Group Commission Report' compiled by the National Literacy Trust (2012).

- Text A is objective and impersonal, as its principal aim is to inform a scholarly reader. The language is formal and technical ('model positive reading behaviour', 'motivation and attainment', 'male reading role models'). It uses cautious language to avoid overgeneralisation ('this is not necessarily the case', 'may have', 'may be'). The factual content is supported by reference to academic sources, presented according to academic conventions.

- Text B is very lively and colourful, as one of its principal aims is to engage the attention of a general, non-expert reader and keep their interest. Some phrases ('bursts of intense activity') are vivid and expressive, and would be unlikely to appear in a more academic text. The author uses informal language ('dads and lads', 'chill out', 'would be cool too') which readers may relate to more readily than they might if the language were more formal. Assertions are made without supporting evidence, as the author is writing from a personal point of view, drawing upon her experiences as a teacher ('Boys in general thrive on competition', 'The best role models seem to be dads, sports coaches and athletes').

- Text C is neither very formal nor very informal in tone. Its aim is to inform and educate the general public and politicians, so it is generally clear and accessible to a non-expert reader. The language is persuasive and opinions are expressed, although in this paragraph they are not supported by specific references to research. However, the report was produced following investigations which included a research review. The text includes recommendations and these are expressed forcefully ('reading for pleasure needs to be an integral element', 'teachers need to be supported'), in contrast to the more cautious manner of Text A. The use of 'there is a specific danger' also marks the text out as less formal than Text A.

The formal style that characterises Text A (and parts of C) will be discussed in this section, and there will be guidance on how to avoid some of the informal features in Text B (and parts of C).

Other characteristics of academic writing such as the use of cautious language to indicate stance, and the role of references are discussed in other chapters of this book.

Task

Word choice

Look at the words below. What do they have in common? What differentiates them?

> minor juvenile paediatric kid bairn brat
> suckling offspring infant child

CROSS
REFERENCE

Chapter 3,
Referring to
sources

Discussion: word choice

These are all words associated with children, but they differ in terms of style and common usage. Language style can be broadly categorised as follows:

FORMAL	NEUTRAL	INFORMAL
infant	child	kid

Formal language can include specialised or technical terms, for example, technical words such as 'offspring', and legal words such as 'minor' and 'juvenile'. In education, the term 'pupil' is commonly used.

So context is everything, and the university context requires specific language use. The language of academic writing can be neutral or formal, and it often includes specialised or technical terms. You must be careful to avoid informal, colloquial language like 'kid', including dialect words like 'bairn' (used in Scotland and some areas of Northern England), and slang words, especially those with derogatory associations, such as 'brat'. You should also be careful with some formal words, particularly those which are quite literary in nature. For example, the word 'suckling' can be used to describe a baby who has not yet been weaned, but this is the kind of word you would expect to find in Shakespeare rather than an academic paper. Dictionaries often provide information on the special characteristics of words.

CROSS
REFERENCE

Appendix 1,
English
language
references

Top tips

Using a thesaurus

A thesaurus can be a useful tool, but like any tool, it requires careful use. You should avoid unthinking reliance on the information it provides: the terms listed in a thesaurus as synonyms are often not exact synonyms, and there is often a lack of information on the style or usage of the term. For example, a thesaurus may provide the following synonyms for the word 'old':

> elderly geriatric senile aged ancient decrepit venerable hoary over the hill

CROSS REFERENCE

Chapter 2, Coherent texts and arguments, Referring back in the text: repetition, variation and pronoun use

However, only the first three are appropriate for academic use, and even they have very specific uses: 'elderly' is more polite than 'old'; 'geriatric' is a technical term common in medical use; 'senile' can refer to the loss of mental faculties (though it can also be used in an insulting way in everyday slang). The other words would sound inappropriate, strange or disturbing in an academic essay!

Before you use a word you have never used before, check in a good dictionary to find out information on usage and to see authentic examples containing the word. And remember that a synonym may not be the best choice; repeating the same word may help the reader more.

Also, note that some terms used in an educational environment may not even feature in a general thesaurus, for example, the term 'early years', which is a term commonly used by educators in relation to children from birth to five years old.

> Training in early years education is needed.

> Early years providers must follow the EYFS curriculum.

It is clear that some words should be avoided completely. However, a lot of language use is a matter of choice. You can often choose between a neutral word and a more formal word. Both will often be acceptable in an academic essay, but the more formal choice may well enhance your writing.

Task

Identifying inappropriate language

Cross out the terms in the lists below which would be inappropriate in an academic essay because they are too informal or literary. It may be necessary to consult a dictionary for one or two of the words.

1) male/man/bloke

2) inebriated/tipsy/drunk

3) impecunious/poor/broke

4) food/nutrition/grub

5) sleep/slumber/doze

Task

Identifying formal language

Identify the more formal choice in the sentences below.

1) <u>Not much/Little</u> research has been carried out on the topic of the effective teaching of spelling.

2) The pupils' performance <u>deteriorated/got worse</u> during Year 7.

3) Alec Clegg <u>got/was awarded</u> a knighthood for his services to education.

4) There are <u>about/approximately</u> thirty pupils in the class.

5) Teachers are required to <u>adhere/keep</u> to the ethical principles <u>enshrined within/contained in</u> Teachers' Standards.

6) Teachers should <u>show/demonstrate</u> a capacity for empathy.

7) It is important to <u>ensure/make sure</u> that children are safe in school.

8) The child requires support <u>such as/like</u> help with reading.

9) Building standards for new schools need to <u>get better/improve</u>.

10) A range of strategies can be employed to <u>facilitate/help</u> learning.

11) <u>More and more/An increasing number of</u> schools offer some form of outdoor education.

12) There are <u>a lot of/many</u> studies on the effects of diet on pupil health.

Strategies for making your writing more formal

1) Avoid conversational expressions such as 'actually', 'by the way' or 'to be honest'.

2) Use the formal negatives, 'little/few', rather than the more conversational 'not much/not many':

   little time/effort/pleasure (uncountable nouns)
   few pupils/schools/experts (countable nouns)

3) It is grammatically correct to start a sentence with 'and' or 'but', and you will find sentences like this in academic texts. However, if you start too many sentences with these words, your style will seem too chatty and unstructured, so make good use of more formal options such as 'in addition' and 'however'.

4) Place adverbs before the main verb (rather than at the beginning or the end of a sentence, as is common in spoken English):

   Originally, the National Curriculum was developed by committees.
   → The National Curriculum was originally developed by committees.

5) Academic discourse aims to be objective. For this reason, care should be taken with the use of personalised language, including personal pronouns such as 'I/you/we'. There may be some situations in which you are expected to write in a personal style, for example, in a reflective essay, where you are required to

discuss your thought processes etc; also, some academic journals, in medicine and psychology for example, have made the conscious decision to adopt a more direct style (eg the use of 'we', as in sentences such as 'We selected fifty samples', instead of passive constructions like 'Fifty samples were selected'). It is therefore necessary to consider each situation in isolation before making a choice about the type of language required. As far as academic assignments are concerned, most will require you to use impersonal structures such as those below:

You can see a comparison of pupil outcomes in Table 2.
→ A comparison of pupil outcomes can be seen in Table 2.
I think this approach is preferable.
→ There is evidence to support this approach (Cross, 2011; Turner, 2015).

6) Avoid contractions like 'they're', 'he's' and 'can't'. You will find contractions in many academic textbooks (occasionally in this one), as the writers want to make them accessible, but they are not felt to be appropriate in academic essays or scholarly journals.

CROSS
REFERENCE

Colons

7) Be cautious with informal punctuation such as dashes (–) and exclamation marks (!). Dashes are sometimes used as a type of parenthesis (as an alternative to brackets), but colons can often provide a more formal alternative:

The problems faced by many rural schools in third world countries – a lack of trained teachers, basic equipment and supplies, and the physical distance between some schools and the populations they serve – are covered in the report.
→ The report covers the problems faced by many rural schools in third world countries: a lack of trained teachers, basic equipment and supplies, and the physical distance between some schools and the populations they serve.

Task

Improving style

Rewrite the text below so that it is more formal and academic in style.

The strong economy means that fewer and fewer people want to be teachers and a lot of schools are struggling. They often don't get help from on high and they're facing cuts all the time.

If schools don't get more money from the Government, they will not be able to deliver good education. There are lots of great teachers out there who do a fantastic job, but all they get in return is criticism in some newspapers and from some politicians.

It's high time people realised that there won't be any good teachers left if things don't get better and schools don't get lots more money to pay their wages.

Top tips

Using the Academic Word List

The **Academic Word List** (Coxhead, 2000) is a list of words which have a high frequency in English-language academic texts. The words at the top end of the list, ie the most frequent, include:

analyse approach area assume benefit concept consistent context data established evidence factor identified indicate involved issue major method occur procedure process role significant specific theory variable

You can check if a word you want to use is on the list at: www.victoria.ac.nz/lals/resources/academicwordlist/

Grammar, spelling and punctuation

When lecturers read and assess your work, they are not looking for perfection. They will overlook occasional minor errors, as long as they do not interfere with the readability of the text or obscure the meaning. However, it is very hard to get high marks if there are numerous grammar, spelling or punctuation errors in your writing, even if the content is good. The standard of your English also has implications for professional practice: the Teachers' Standard 3 demands that you 'demonstrate an understanding of and take responsibility for promoting high standards of literacy, articulacy and the correct use of standard English, whatever the teacher's specialist subject'.

English grammar, spelling and punctuation can be a challenge both for students whose first language is not English and for some native speakers. In the UK, educational attitudes towards the explicit teaching of grammar to school children have varied greatly over the last few decades. Whatever the rights and wrongs of this, one of the outcomes is that some people in the UK may have learned very little about grammar at school. And even those who did may feel a bit hazy about some of the rules and terminology. In order to meet the standards necessary for academic success, it is necessary to grasp certain grammatical concepts. This section provides explanations and examples which will help students who lack confidence in this area. You will find more detailed explanations and examples of grammatical terms used in this chapter (in **bold** in the text) in Appendix 2.

Sometimes, errors are down to insufficient proofreading, rather than a lack of knowledge. It is essential that you leave yourself enough time to read through your finished essay or report several times, firstly to make sure that it is readable and makes sense, and secondly to proofread and pick up 'typos' (typing errors), grammar, spelling and punctuation slips, or messy formatting.

CROSS REFERENCE

Communication Skills for your Education Degree

CROSS REFERENCE

Appendix 2, Grammatical terminology

CROSS REFERENCE

Chapter 5, Preparing your work for submission, Editing and proofreading your final text

Common areas of difficulty in grammar and spelling

There are a number of areas of grammar and spelling that cause particular problems.

Quantifiers

Quantifiers are words used before **nouns** (terms used for people, places or things) to indicate number or amount.

- The quantifier 'fewer' is used with **countable nouns** (literally things which can be counted, usually ending in 's' in English):

  less pupils/teachers/schools ✘
  fewer pupils/teachers/schools ✓

- The quantifier 'less' is used with **uncountable nouns** (things seen as a mass which cannot be split or counted):

  less effort/time/money/work

- The quantifier 'amount' should only be used with uncountable nouns:

  a large amount of teachers ✘
  a large number of teachers ✓
  a large amount of documentation ✓

Grammatical agreement

- Most **sentences** in English contain a **main clause** which is built upon two basic elements: a **subject**, and a **verb** which agrees with it:

  The lesson [subject] was [verb] successful.

  Many of the schools mentioned in the select committee's report [subject] are situated [verb] in densely populated urban areas.

  Be careful to make sure a verb agrees with its subject; it is quite easy to get this wrong if the main word in the subject and the verb are far apart, and if there are other nouns between the subject and verb:

  One of the most difficult challenges faced by teachers working full-time are maintaining work–life balance. ✘

  One of the most difficult challenges faced by teachers working full-time is maintaining work–life balance. ✓

- **Nouns** can sometimes be replaced with **pronouns** (short words such as 'he/it/them'). These pronouns must also agree with the noun they refer to:

  Information is supplied on the tests and on how it is administered. ✘
  Information is supplied on the tests and on how they are administered. ✓
  The tests are prepared by groups of educators. This is given to schools in May. ✘
  The tests are prepared by groups of educators. They are given to schools in May. ✓

Commonly confused words

Many errors in students' written work arise because of confusion between certain words.

- Be careful to distinguish between 'there' and 'their'. The former introduces the theme of the sentence, or signifies place; the latter denotes possession:

    <u>There</u> are many issues affecting pupil performance.

    Teachers have to be aware of <u>their</u> own needs too.

- Do not confuse 'effect' (noun) and 'affect' (verb):

    Teacher workload can have a profound <u>effect</u> on both teachers and their pupils.

    Teacher workload can <u>affect</u> both teachers and their pupils profoundly.

    There is a verb 'effect', but it has another meaning (to make happen, bring about), and is usually restricted to particular nouns such as 'change':

    A number of teachers reported that they felt powerless to effect change in their schools.

- Be careful to distinguish between **singular** and **plural** with the following words:

    a recent <u>phenomenon</u> (singular)

    the study of several <u>phenomena</u> important to teaching (plural)

    provide evidence of practice related to each <u>criterion</u> (singular)

    meet all the <u>criteria</u> (plural)

- Differentiate between the following **noun** and **verb** spellings:

NOUN *–ice*	VERB *–ise*
advice	advise
device	devise
practice	practise
licence	license

CROSS REFERENCE

Chapter 2, Coherent texts and arguments, Referring back in the text: repetition, variation and pronoun use

Task

Commonly confused words

Choose the correct form of the word in the sentences below.

1) New government policy has implications for teaching <u>practice/practise</u>.

2) The policy affects the ability of teachers to <u>practice/practise</u> effectively.

3) Pupils were offered <u>advice/advise</u> on nutrition.

4) Teachers can <u>advice/advise</u> on completion of homework.

5) An interactive whiteboard is a useful <u>device/devise</u> for sharing texts

6) The curriculum guidelines have been <u>deviced/devised</u> by the DfE.

7) Public houses are <u>licenced/licensed</u> to sell alcohol.

8) Applicants must possess a valid driving <u>licence/license</u>.

9) The paper reported on the <u>affects/effects</u> of the bad weather.

10) Several schools were <u>affected/effected</u> by the strike.

11) The teachers planned <u>there/their</u> lessons together.

12) <u>There/Their</u> is no proposal for a change in the curriculum.

Note that US English uses 'practice' and 'license' for both noun and verb.

Common areas of difficulty in punctuation

There are some strict rules governing punctuation in English; these rules are largely tied up with English grammar rules, such as the use of commas with relative clauses (discussed later in this section). However, in other cases, there are choices available to you; these choices are a question of style, but they are still important as they can affect clarity and readability. Some important punctuation rules and choices are discussed below.

The apostrophe

If you have problems with apostrophes, you are not alone! David Crystal, a well-known linguistics scholar, cites apostrophe use as one of the most problematic aspects of the English language: 'Another day when the phone doesn't stop ringing, and (once again) all because of the apostrophe' (Crystal, 2012). It is a topic which clearly exercises the general British public, judging by the number of letters sent to newspapers to complain of apostrophe misuse! However, there are some simple rules which can help.

- After a **singular noun**, or a **proper noun** (like a name), **'s** is used to denote possession:
  in this child's best interests
  Jeremy Corbyn's policy on education

  After **plural nouns**, and **proper nouns** ending in **s**, the apostrophe comes after the **s**:
  The boys' changing room/Robert Burns' poetry.
  Note that some plurals are not made by adding -s or -es. For example, the plural of 'child' is 'children'. When making children possessive we use 'children's'.
  It is also acceptable to add a possessive **s** in this case, as in 'Burns's book', but be consistent.
  Be careful with irregular plurals not ending in s – the apostrophe comes before the possessive **s**.
  the children's parents

- Apostrophes also signal missing letters in **contractions** like 'can't' (cannot), 'doesn't' (does not) and 'they'll' (they will).

  Do not confuse words which sound the same but have different meanings, grammar and spelling:
  − 'it's' is the contracted form of 'it is/has', whereas 'its' is a **possessive pronoun** like 'my' or 'her':
  The school provided details of its policy on staff development.
  It's hot today.

— 'your' is a possessive pronoun, while 'you're' is a contraction of 'you are':

Always wash your hands.

You're late.

— 'they're' is a contraction of 'they are', distinct from 'there' and 'their'

There is pressure on schools to stay within their budgets.

They're here!

You will avoid this problem if you write, as you should in academic writing, without using contractions.

Hyphens

Multi-word **adjectives** (words which describe nouns), such as the first word of this sentence, are usually hyphenated when they come before a noun, but not when they come after:

- an out-of-date educational practice
- an educational practice which is out of date
- a three-day-old baby
- a baby who is three days old

Brackets

Brackets should be used sparingly as they can interrupt the flow of a text. If you do use them, be aware of the rules.

- If the bracketed information is part of the sentence, it requires no specific punctuation:

  The data (collected over a three-month period) revealed a significant improvement in pupil performance.

The brackets here could be replaced with commas or perhaps dashes (though dashes are a little on the informal side).

- If the brackets contain a separate sentence, it should be punctuated as such:

  The data revealed a significant improvement in pupil performance. (The data was collected over a three-month period.) Several teachers noted attitudes to school.

In cases like this, brackets are just one choice available for reducing the focus on this piece of information. Other choices include:

  The data, which was collected over a three-month period, revealed a significant improvement in pupil performance.

Punctuation and sentence structure

The use of full stops, commas, colons and semi-colons is intrinsically linked with the control of sentence structure in English. Some of the most important rules and patterns are detailed below. Some example sentences in this section are authentic examples from academic education textbooks.

Full stops

Full stops are the most straightforward of punctuation marks and they do not really cause problems for students (although their misuse is linked with 'fragments' and 'run-ons', discussed later in this section). Suffice it to say that they are the main way of indicating the boundaries between **sentences**.

> A teacher will usually be observed teaching once a term. This monitoring can benefit both the teacher and the school.

Commas

> Commas are the equivalent of changing gear when driving; you come to a point where you need to slow down a little or turn a corner. The commas help you negotiate these changes, but also, and perhaps more importantly, they enable you to take your reader along with you.
>
> (Peck and Coyle, 2012, p 54)

So commas can be a way of guiding, or 'driving', your reader through the text. Below are some common patterns in comma use.

- It can make a sentence easier to read if the parts of a **sentence** which come before, after, or in the middle of the main idea are separated with commas, especially in longer sentences:

> According to research by Andrews et al (2007), grammar is learned most effectively when it is taught through reading and writing.

> As a teacher, you will be expected to form good relationships with your colleagues as well as with your class.

> Jolliffe, who is a leading expert in the field, advocates a cooperative learning approach.

> SATs can be stressful for pupils, with some parents deciding to take holidays rather than send their children to school during assessment periods.

These commas are not obligatory, and some people prefer not to use them too much as they believe they 'clutter up' the text. When you have a choice like this, let it be motivated by sensitivity to the experience of the reader. Will a comma help the reader navigate the text more easily and focus on the most important information in the sentence?

- It is not obligatory to use a comma before 'and/but/or' when using them to join words or parts of a sentence, but it can often help to make long sentences easier to read. Again, be sensitive to the experience of the reader. In the first example below, the comma before 'but' helps break up a complex sentence with many grammatical elements into two discernible ideas; in the second example, commas signal the three items in the list introduced by the colon ('giving', 'providing', 'offering'), the second 'and' thus clearly forming part of the third item:

> Traditionally, working with children with disabilities has been seen as a less attractive career pathway in comparison to other aspects of education, but in reality it is a rewarding and challenging sphere of education which has increased in importance.

> As a teacher, you will need to be proactive in involving parents in their children's literacy development: giving explanations, providing materials, and offering advice and strategies for support with homework.

- The **main clause** (the main idea in a sentence) is usually separated with a comma from a **participle clause** (an '–ing' or '–ed' verb form adding information). This comma is not obligatory, but it can help the reader to follow a long sentence:

  > All teachers need to work with a range of agencies, actively involving and respecting the contribution of others to the education and welfare of the pupils they teach.

- Another clause can also be added to a **main clause** with a linking **conjunction** such as 'although/because/whilst'. These two parts of the sentence can be separated with a comma, especially when the main clause follows the other clause:

  > Whilst every effort was made to avoid a timetable clash, it was not possible to teach both mathematics and science on the same day.

- Commas are not used before **that-clauses** (structures following certain verbs etc):

  > Teachers recognise, that a good classroom is vital if a productive learning environment is to be created and sustained. ✗
  > Teachers recognise that a good classroom is vital if a productive learning environment is to be created and sustained. ✓

- Do not use commas directly in between a **subject** and **verb**, no matter how long the subject:

  > The assessment of children's ability to spell accurately, is now a feature of annual testing. ✗
  > The assessment of children's ability to spell accurately is now a feature of annual testing. ✓

Task

Variation in comma use

The two texts below are well written and do not break any punctuation rules. However, they differ in their use of commas. This may be due to individual choice, or editorial policy (they are both from textbooks).

What differences in comma use can you find? Which style do you prefer? Why?

A

However, recent research (James & Engelhardt, 2012) has shown that the act of writing causes us to engage more deeply with ideas and thus to remember more of what has been said or copied, since writing is not simply a physical process – it is what Berninger & Graham (1998) and Berninger & Amtmann (2004) term 'language by hand'. Other research suggests that encouraging children to write with digital devices changes the emphasis of what is written to a more superficial emphasis on the presentation of visual ideas and extra features at the expense of their deeper significance for individual children; a process known as 'feature overload' in general terms (Olchowka, 2014), and as cognitive redundancy in terms of the specific effects of particular media (Gleaves & Walker, 2013). Yet other research suggests that handwriting enables pupils to be more creative with their ideas, on the basis that with a digital device, children are hindered by the limitations of the software or the user-interface.

(Walker and Gleaves, 2015)

B

Retelling has been shown to be an effective learning strategy. The National Literacy Trust (2012) found that children in the long term retained as much as 90% of information by explaining what they have learnt to each other or an adult. This requires children to understand a concept before they explain it to others but it clearly shows the benefit of retelling in order to fully retain what has been learnt.

Retelling is probably the most common method of speaking activity used in schools. In the Early Years retelling stories happens frequently, but it is important to continue this throughout the school. Retelling techniques such as stories through puppets, character studies in costume, events through figures, and experiences through pictures would, therefore, be of benefit for every class in the primary school.

(Bushnell, 2015)

Colons

CROSS REFERENCE

Parallel structures

Colons are used to introduce something that expands in some way on what precedes it, by, for example, providing an explanation, or listing items:

We read in a very different way when we are researching a subject we plan to write about: we are looking for what is relevant to our topic, and for answers to questions we have.

(Allott, 2015)

Semi-colons

CROSS REFERENCE

Parallel structures

A semi-colon can be used instead of a full stop to separate **sentences** which are closely connected.

Writing frames provide a series of prompts or sentence starters which provide a framework for a piece of writing; they can be very helpful if used flexibly.

(Allott, 2015)

Focus on fragments and run-on sentences

It has been established that most **sentences** in English contain a **main clause** which contains two basic elements: a **subject** and a **verb** which agrees with it:

Teaching [subject] is [verb] a profession within the education sector.

School teachers [subject] are [verb] vital to their schools and communities.

If a sentence is lacking a main clause, or if a main clause is lacking a subject or a main verb, the sentence is incomplete, ie it is a 'fragment':

While the majority reported a fall in standards. ✗ (no main clause)

While the majority reported a fall in standards, a small number improved considerably. ✓

Immigrants' integration into schools and communities. ✗ (no verb)

Immigrants have been integrated into schools and communities. ✓

Lately, have admitted pupils in large numbers. ✗ (no subject)

Lately, rural schools in Lincolnshire have admitted pupils in large numbers. ✓

If there is more than one subject/verb structure, they should be separated by full stops or semi-colons, or connected (with **conjunctions**, for example). If only a comma is used, it creates a 'run-on sentence', which is grammatically incorrect:

School teachers are vital to their schools and communities, they provide both education and pastoral support. ✗

School teachers are vital to their schools and communities; they provide both education and pastoral support. ✓

School teachers are vital to their schools and communities, and they provide both education and pastoral support. ✓

Run-on sentences also include those beginning with words and phrases used to connect two sentences such as 'however/therefore/as a result':

Psychology is a central part of undergraduate education curricula in the UK, however, student teachers report difficulties recognising its relevance and value. ✗

Psychology is a central part of undergraduate education curricula in the UK. However, student teachers report difficulties recognising its relevance and value. ✓

Psychology is a central part of undergraduate education curricula in the UK; however, student teachers report difficulties recognising its relevance and value. ✓

Focus on 'hanging participles' (sometimes known as 'dangling participles')

As discussed above, it is common to attach a **participle clause** to a main clause. However, it is important to make sure that the two parts of such a sentence are clearly connected.

Being prone to failure, teachers are expected to pay particular attention to these pupils. ✗

Being prone to failure, these pupils require particular attention from teachers. ✓

Admitted with a history of disruptive behaviour, the headteacher assessed the pupil. ✗

Admitted with a history of disruptive behaviour, the pupil was assessed by the headteacher. ✓

In the examples marked as incorrect, it is as if the teacher or headteacher are being described by the first clause.

This can also happen with other phrases, creating a certain ambiguity in the example below:

> Without an understanding of what their intervention entails, teachers cannot help parents to support their children. ✗

> Without an understanding of what their intervention entails, parents cannot be helped to support their children. ✓

Focus on relative clauses

The pronouns 'that' and 'which' are used to refer back to nouns in what are called 'relative clauses'. These are very common in academic writing because they are very useful for defining terms and adding information to the main topic of a sentence. However, the rules are quite complicated and mistakes are quite common. In brief, 'that' and 'which' can both be used to refer back to something which is being defined or restricted in some way (restrictive/defining relative clauses); 'that' or 'who' are used for people. There are no commas in this case:

> The tablet computer is a device that/which can be used in a variety of ways in the classroom. (defining; one type of device)

> Specialised knowledge is required for teachers who/that work with children with English as an additional language. (restricted subset of teachers)

Only 'which' (or 'who' for people) can be used when adding extra information (non-restrictive/non-defining relative clauses) which relates to the whole group or idea, not a subset. This type of clause can be removed from the sentence without making the sentence ungrammatical. Commas must be used in these sentences:

> Teachers are encouraged to set both short-term and long-term goals, which can be adapted as they get to know their classes.

> One approach to early reading development is systematic synthetic phonics (SSP), which is widely used in English schools.

> Recently qualified primary teachers, who are trained in teaching SSP, are well placed to contribute to schools' development of phonics teaching.

Refining grammar and punctuation

Task

Grammar and punctuation

1) Punctuate the text below so that it makes sense.

Making statements into questions

Word order mentioned earlier can also be important in English when we want to make a statement into a question sometimes we do not need to change the order at all for example

You want some tea.
You want some tea?

Here the change from a full stop to a question mark at the end of the sentence changes the way we say the sentence and what it means in spoken language we have in recent years become used to the so-called 'interrogative intonation' often through exposure to Australian soaps such as *Neighbours* and *Home and Away* this means the way in which the voice rising at the end of a sentence can often make a simple declarative sentence sound like a question 'I come from Sydney?' interestingly this pattern of rising tone is similar in many languages including french german spanish and dialects of mandarin chinese

(Adapted from Waugh et al, 2016, p 156)

2) Correct the grammar and punctuation mistakes in the text below.

Media literacy

An Ofcom survey of children's media use in 2014 showed that in the UK childrens' use of a variety of devices to go online are increasing at home (Ofcom, 2014). That use could be for a variety of purposes and whilst the report does not look specifically at children writing digitally. It does provide an insight into activities which almost certainly include digital writing. Clearly text messaging, is a significant part of that and it is probably safe to assume, that the 32% of 8 to 11-year-olds what owns a phone will use text messages. And the 20% what owns smartphones, may also use those for email or other text creation.

(Adapted from Bennett, 2015)

Top tips

Spelling and grammar check

Use a spell and grammar tool, but always double-check that the suggestion given to you makes sense, as these computer programmes cannot recognise some subtleties of usage, especially in grammar. Also, make sure your spell and grammar check is set to UK English, as there are a number of differences between UK and US English, and it is important to be consistent.

	UK	US
–ise v –ize	prioritise, recognise	prioritize, recognize*
–our v –or	colour, behaviour	color; behavior
–re v –er	centre, metre	center, meter
–ll– v –l–	travelling, cancelled	traveling, canceled

*The 'z' spelling is also acceptable in UK English; just be consistent.

Parallel structures

Parallel structures are formed when there is repetition of words, phrases, grammatical structures and punctuation patterns (combined with contrasting elements which move the text forward). They are common in academic writing because they are useful tools for organising information clearly, particularly when comparing and contrasting, or when listing items. Note how these structures often include colons and semi-colons as organisational tools, eg:

> Schön (1983) distinguishes between <u>reflection on action</u> and <u>reflection in action</u>. <u>Reflecting *on* action</u> happens <u>after the event</u>, <u>reflection *in* action</u> <u>during the event</u>. <u>Reflection on action is</u> a prerequisite to becoming <u>a competent practitioner</u>; <u>reflection in action</u>, on the other hand, <u>is</u> a deeper skill that is essential if you are to become <u>a capable practitioner</u>.
>
> (Pryjmachuk, 2011c, p 67)

There are many elements which contribute to the profile of a successful reader. Two key aspects of reading are <u>language comprehension</u> and <u>word recognition</u>. These are encapsulated in the *Simple View of Reading* (Rose, 2005). Although both aspects are necessary for success, <u>some children will need to be given more support with language comprehension</u>, while <u>others will require greater support with word recognition</u>.

An understanding of the *Simple View of Reading* enables teachers to identify children's learning needs and helps them to develop a profile of individuals. There are four main types of reader: <u>those who</u> require support with both <u>language comprehension and word recognition</u>; <u>those who</u> are strong in both <u>language comprehension and word recognition</u>; <u>those who</u> have good <u>language comprehension</u> but weaker <u>word recognition</u>; and <u>those who</u> have weak <u>language comprehension</u> but stronger <u>word recognition</u>.

Notice how the *repetition* of certain phrases and structures highlights the information which is *different*, eg 'strong' v 'weak'; 'language comprehension' and 'word recognition'. This combination of repetition and change makes the text very easy to process for the reader (McIntyre, 1997).

Be careful to avoid 'faulty parallelism', ie when items in a list do not share the same grammar:

> An understanding of the *Simple View of Reading* enables teachers to identify children's learning needs and in helping them to develop a profile of individuals. There are four main types of reader: those who require support with both language comprehension and word recognition; some are strong in both language comprehension and word recognition; having good language comprehension but weaker word recognition; and weak in language comprehension but stronger word recognition. ✗

Task

Parallel structures

Use the notes below to write short texts using parallel structures. Think about how you might use commas, colons and semi-colons to organise the information.

1) diagnosing reading problems – impact – pupil/class/school

2) initiative – working with parents – help/guidance/support

3) aims – improve pupil outcomes/child development/involvement of fathers as well as mothers/support for looked-after children

4) pupils with English as an additional language (EAL) – social engagement/possible previous traumatic experiences/extent of prior school attendance in country of origin/parental understanding of English

Summary

This chapter has analysed elements of academic style and provided strategies to help you write clear, accurate English for academic purposes. It has outlined the choices available to you in terms of expression, grammatical structures and punctuation, as you complete your written assignments. In addition, it has outlined some of the most challenging areas of English grammar and punctuation, in order to help you avoid common errors and refine your writing. Good style and accuracy will help you to create a good impression in your writing, and allow your ideas to shine through.

Sources of example texts

Bennett, J (2015) Beyond Pen and Paper. In Waugh, D, Neaum, S and Bushnell, A (eds) *Beyond Early Writing*. Northwich: Critical Publishing.

Bushnell, A (2015) Finding a Written Voice. In Waugh, D, Neaum, S and Bushnell, A (eds) *Beyond Early Writing*. Northwich: Critical Publishing.

Marsh, S (2015) How Can We Encourage Boys to Read for Pleasure? Teachers Give Their Views. *The Guardian.* [online] Available at: www.theguardian.com/teacher-network/2015/jun/11/how-can-we-encourage-boys-to-read-for-pleasure-teachers-give-their-views (accessed 24 March 2018).

National Literacy Trust (2012) *The Report of the All-Party Parliamentary Literacy Group Commission: Report Compiled by the National Literacy Trust.* London: National Literacy Trust.

Walker, C and Gleaves, A (2015) Beyond Longhand: The Mentality and Physicality of Writing by Hand. In Waugh, D, Neaum, S and Bushnell, A (eds) *Beyond Early Writing*. Northwich: Critical Publishing.

References

Academic Word List. [online] Available at: www.victoria.ac.nz/lals/resources/academicwordlist (accessed 2 April 2017).

Coxhead, A (2000) A New Academic Wordlist. *TESOL Quarterly*, 34, 213–38.

Crystal, D (2012) On Waterstone(')s. *DCBLOG*. [online] Available at: http://david-crystal.blogspot.co.uk/2012/01/on-waterstones.html (accessed 2 April 2017).

McIntyre, M (1997) Lucidity and Science I: Writing Skills and the Pattern Perception Hypothesis. *Interdisciplinary Science Reviews*, 22, 199–216.

Peck, J and Coyle, M (2012) *Write it Right: The Secrets of Effective Writing*. 2nd ed. New York: Palgrave Macmillan.

Chapter 5
Preparing your work for submission

This chapter will help you to assess if a piece of work is ready to be submitted. It offers advice on the final edit of your text, including proofreading. It provides you with information and guidance on formatting and presentation. It also presents the options available to you if you feel you need further professional support with your writing.

Are you ready to submit your work?

When lecturers mark your work, they refer very closely to assessment guidelines and marking descriptors. It is therefore very important that you pay equally close attention to these documents. You should use these as the starting point for your assessment, and as a kind of 'checklist' at the end of the writing process, before you submit. The next section covers some of the most important considerations when preparing your work for submission.

Have you done what you were asked to do?

Have you stuck to the word count?

You will most certainly be penalised if you either *fail to meet* or *exceed* the specified word count. Word counts are not arbitrary numbers plucked out of the air. They are decided on with a range of factors in mind.

- Word counts ensure equity since all students are given the same limit.
- Written assignments need to be a certain length in order to allow for the inclusion of a substantial amount of detail and/or a substantive argument.
- Word counts can be used to differentiate between different levels of study: for example, a third-year student should be expected to produce more writing on a given topic than a first-year student.
- Word limits require students to be selective in their response to a task, demonstrating their judgement regarding the most important aspects of a topic.
- Word limits require students to avoid redundancy (repetition of information or unnecessary repetition of words).
- Word limits require students to write concisely, to avoid 'wordiness'.

Most universities allow you a 10 per cent leeway either side (this is what 'plus or minus 10 per cent' means), so a 2,500 word assignment needs to be between 2,250 (2,500 – 250) and 2,750 (2,500 + 250) words. One side of A4, typed in a standard font (say Arial 12pt) and using double line spacing, normally contains between 250 and 300 words; so you can get a rough idea of how many words you have got by multiplying the number of pages by this figure. For example, if you have typed 11 pages, you will have around 2,750–3,300 words in total. The word count usually excludes your reference list, but double-check with the module leader if this is not mentioned in the assessment guidelines.

Are you clear about the submission process?

Checklist

CROSS
REFERENCE

Presentation

- Are you required to submit a hard copy or to upload your document via your VLE? (You may need to do both.)
- If submitting a hard copy, how many copies do you need to submit, and in what form (eg A4, printed on one side or on both sides, secured in a folder or stapled)?
- Do you need to complete and attach a **standard cover sheet**? Or are you expected to create your own cover sheet? (You may be able to do both.)
- Where do you need to hand in hard copies (eg the school office, the office of a particular member of staff)?
- If submitting online, do you know the exact procedure? Make sure you find out about this in good time. Perhaps ask the module lecturer if it is possible to do a practice submission beforehand. (Many lecturers arrange an unassessed

formative assignment and practice submission early in the course, so make sure you take advantage of such an opportunity.)

- Are you required to make your submission anonymous? (This is usually the case.) If so, have you been careful to make sure your name is not visible? Have you included your student number?

- Ensure you know the *exact* deadline for submission (including any personal deadlines or extensions you may have been given); electronic systems may deny a submission, or flag it up as late, at 4:01pm if the deadline is 4:00pm.

Editing and proofreading your final text

Before you hand in the final version of your text, you need to read through it with two separate aims in mind. The first type of reading should be a type of **final editing**, where you focus on meaning and flow, making sure that everything hangs together and makes sense. The second type of reading is **proofreading**, where you check the text for surface errors in spelling, grammar and punctuation. This is also an opportunity to pick up on any problems with typing or formatting. Many students overlook the first type of reading (a final edit of content, organisation and meaning), and focus purely on looking for mistakes. However, it is important to do both. The two processes will obviously overlap: while reading to check meaning, you might also catch a few mistakes; while proofreading, you might encounter a possible ambiguity, for instance. This is to be expected, but you should take care not to be distracted from your principal aim.

Editing your final text

Make sure you leave enough time to read through your work several times to ensure that another person reading your essay will be able to follow what you have said and understand the points you want to make.

Top tips

The final edit

- Reading out loud can help you put yourself in the reader's shoes and get a good sense of the flow and naturalness of the text.
- Trying to read the same text over and over is difficult to do, as your brain tends to switch off. Read it once, then put the text aside and go for a walk or make a cup of tea. You will come back to the text with fresh eyes.

CROSS
REFERENCE

Chapter 2,
Coherent
texts and
arguments,
Editing and
redrafting for
coherence

Systematic treatment of names and titles

In education, you will often be required to refer to terms such as 'dyslexia' or 'attention deficit hyperactive disorder', and to the titles of professional organisations, such as the Department for Education or the National Literacy

Trust. When referring to these, it is important to follow the conventions regarding the use of **capitalisation**.

- Most disabilities and conditions are not capitalised, eg dyslexia, autism, attention deficit disorder.
- Conditions named after an individual capitalise the name, eg Asperger's Syndrome.
- The titles of organisations are capitalised, eg the National Curriculum.

Many terms and organisations are also known by their acronyms. An acronym is the short form of a multi-word name, usually formed using the first letter of each word, eg:

- standard assessment tests (SATs)
- key stages (KS)
- modern foreign languages (MFL)
- English as an additional language (EAL)

Or in some cases, parts of key words:

- Office for Standards in Education (Ofsted)

Often, people are more familiar with the acronym than the name, sometimes to the extent that they can be a little hazy on what it actually stands for!

In your writing, it is important to be systematic in your use of names and acronyms. The rule in academic writing is very simple: when you mention a term for the first time, you should use the full name, with the acronym following immediately in parentheses; after this, you should always use the acronym. The following example demonstrates this clearly.

> The 1988 Education Reform Act (ERA) threatened the consensual approach to education policy which had involved government, Local Education Authorities (LEA) and teacher unions. The work of the Schools Council from the 1960s and the Assessment of Performance Unit (APU) from 1975 provided the first indications of the coming national curriculum and the monitoring processes which were to accompany it. LEAs often led the way in supporting schools' response to ERA.
>
> (Adapted from Waugh, 2015, p 10)

CROSS
REFERENCE

Chapter 2,
Coherent
texts and
arguments

Systematic use of names and acronyms adds to the flow and coherence of the text.

Note that acronyms are different from **abbreviations**, which are formed by shortening a word, eg:

- approx (approximately);
- etc (from the Latin 'et cetera', meaning 'and so on').

The fact that something has been abbreviated is often indicated by the full stop at the end (approx., etc.), but this is often omitted (as in this book, for example). The important thing is to be consistent.

Systems for highlighting language

In academic writing, **bold**, *italics* and 'quotation marks' are often used to highlight text in some way. It is important that you are systematic and consistent in your use of these.

Task

Systems for highlighting language

What 'systems' for highlighting language are used by the writers below?

A

The ending -*ee* is an interesting morpheme, originally borrowed from the French in words such as *fiancée, divorcee, employee*, and showing the person to whom something is done. This was followed in English by such coinages as *trainee and nominee*, and more recently by *tutee* (one who is tutored). However, since *tutor* is, strictly speaking, a Latin word, there are those who argue that we should rather speak of a *tutatus*, recalling the words of the journalist C. P. Scott in the 1930s: "Television? The word is half Greek, half Latin. No good can come of it."

(Waugh et al, 2016, p 31)

B

Poems and stories can provide a rich source of invented or 'nonsense' words: words which won't appear in dictionaries (although some do eventually). These texts provide opportunities for children to debate the words' possible meanings, as well as working out how to pronounce them. Poems such as Lewis Carroll's (1871) *The Jabberwocky* ('Twas brillig, and the slithy toves did gyre and gimble in the wabe') and stories like Roald Dahl's *The BFG* (1984) which includes such words as *wopsey, whiffling, glamourly, uckyslush* and *bundongle* are an ideal starting point.

(Jolliffe and Waugh with Carss, 2015, p 173)

C

English lexicon features many words that can cause confusion because they sound like other words but are spelled differently (**homophones** such as *sew, so* and *sow*; *see* and *sea*; *there, their* and *they're*). We also have **homographs**, which are spelled the same but may be pronounced differently and have different meanings (*sow* a seed and *sow*, a female pig; *record* your favourite programme and break a *record*; a dog's *lead* and a *lead* weight). Often, both homographs and homophones are referred to under the general heading of **homonyms** (meaning the same name), although more accurately homonyms are words that are both spelled the same and sound the same, but have different meanings.

(Waugh et al, 2016, p 41)

Discussion: systems for highlighting language

- In A, the writer uses italics for Latin terms and example words, and double quotation marks for a quotation.

- In B, the writer uses italics for unusual words, and single quotation marks to quote from the literature. It is a good idea to reserve one type of quotation mark (single or double) for quotations only; this may be specified in your assessment guidelines, but, if not, just make sure you are consistent.

- In C, the writer uses bold for the first mention of a key term. This is very common in textbooks as it helps students to identify important concepts. Italics are used where examples are given.

Proofreading

Proofreading is the final component of the writing process. It is the process whereby you check the text for surface errors in spelling, grammar and punctuation, and make sure that there are no typing mistakes ('typos') or formatting errors/inconsistencies.

Proofreading is actually a thorny issue. Firstly, students sometimes confuse it with the editing and redrafting process described in Chapter 2 (including the 'final edit' referred to above). In fact, proofreading should only involve the correction of small surface errors; it should not involve changing the meaning or structure of your work.

Secondly, proofreading can be something you do yourself, or it can be something you ask or employ someone else to do. There are no uniform guidelines across UK universities with respect to this process, so it is important that you consider the issues involved carefully. If you decide to employ a professional proofreader, you should first find out if your university offers a proofreading service. If no official services are available, you should seek recommendations from friends or fellow students. When you have made a decision, make sure that you and the proofreader make contact beforehand to discuss the terms of your 'contract'. You should both be very clear on what can be expected. The proofreader can be asked to clean up surface errors in spelling, grammar and punctuation, but they should not be involved in changing the structure or meaning of your work. There are good reasons for this: firstly, universities obviously expect work submitted by students to be their own work in essence (though they accept that students may ask for help with grammar and punctuation); secondly, you do not want your own voice or message to be distorted in any way.

Thirdly, be very clear that anyone who proofreads your work is merely *making suggestions*; it is then up to you to consider these, and to accept or reject them. Ultimately, only you are responsible for your work.

Top tips

Proofreading

- Become adept at proofreading your own writing by noting the kind of errors that have been picked up on in previous assignments, and focusing on these.

- Make use of the spelling and grammar check tool of your word processing program. Microsoft Word will indicate spelling mistakes by underlining them in red, and grammar mistakes by underlining them in green. (These will also help you identify some typing and formatting issues, eg, too many/no spaces between words.) This is a very useful tool, but it is to be treated with caution: it is a computer program, not a human being, and thus, sometimes cannot identify a particular nuance in a text. You need to assess each suggestion carefully.

- You should always be involved in proofreading your own work, but many people, including experienced academics, sometimes ask a peer or colleague to look at their writing. In this way, proofreading can become a type of collaborative activity, one that could enable you to develop a skill that will be essential in future academic studies and your work life. This is distinct from the academic malpractice of collusion, where a student takes credit for work they are not responsible for.

Task

Proofreading practice

Find and correct errors of spelling, grammar, punctuation and formatting in the following texts.

A

It is important when looking at childrens' work to seperate careless mistakes from genuine spelling problems. You may not feel that it is desireable to correct every error in each childs work, but some people would argue that it is not only important but nessessary if each child is to fulfill their potensial. A few miniutes spent helping children to aquire a familliarity with common spellings would'nt go amiss in many classrooms. Unfortuneatly many teachers do not see the value of teaching spelling and its importance is thus diminished in childrens' eyes.

B

Teachers may feel it is alright to quickly scan a peice of work looking for mistakes and then tell a child to check their work, but this practise may not help the child to suppliment his spelling repertoire.

Personally speaking I am of the opinoin that childrens' spelling improves when they percieve spelling as an inportant aspect of writing, but are not afraid to experiment with words and do'nt show any reluctence to make use of a dictionery.

Formatting

CROSS
REFERENCE

*Studying for
your Education
Degree,
Chapter 6,
Assessment*

In written assessments, you will be judged on the breadth of your knowledge, the depth of your understanding, the quality of your ideas and analysis, and the clarity and coherence of your writing. However, even the best work cannot fully impress the reader if it is poorly formatted and presented. Untidy presentation and inconsistent formatting will hinder the reader's ability to navigate your text. It can also suggest a 'sloppy' or unprofessional approach. It is for these reasons that formatting and presentation usually form part of the criteria for assessment in marking descriptors.

The following tasks will help you understand how seemingly minor formatting choices can greatly affect the reader. The subsequent discussions will guide you towards formatting and presenting your work clearly and professionally.

Line spacing

Task

Line spacing

Look at the three versions of work below. What differences do you notice in the formatting of the text? Which version is usually *not* acceptable in university work? Why?

A

Primary education in England has, despite some outward appearances, changed considerably since the 1970s. Schools have acquired some elements of autonomy through devolution of some powers from local authorities, but this is a restricted autonomy, constrained by governmental imposition of testing regimes designed to ensure adherence to the curriculum. The nature of that curriculum has changed repeatedly, with each new government wishing to impose its stamp upon primary education.

B

Primary education in England has, despite some outward appearances,

changed considerably since the 1970s. Schools have acquired some elements

of autonomy through devolution of some powers from local authorities, but

this is a restricted autonomy, constrained by governmental imposition of

testing regimes designed to ensure adherence to the curriculum. The nature of

that curriculum has changed repeatedly, with each new government wishing

to impose its stamp upon primary education.

C

Primary education in England has, despite some outward appearances, changed considerably since the 1970s. Schools have acquired some elements of autonomy through devolution of some powers from local authorities, but this is a restricted autonomy, constrained by governmental imposition of testing regimes designed to ensure adherence to the curriculum. The nature of that curriculum has changed repeatedly, with each new government wishing to impose its stamp upon primary education.

Discussion: line spacing

The three texts have been formatted with different line spacing. A is **single-spaced**, B is **1.5 spaced**, and C is **double-spaced**. (In Microsoft Word, line spacing is adjusted through the 'paragraph' tool on the toolbar.) Assessment guidelines usually specify the line spacing you should use. Most guidelines specify 1.5 or double spaced, for two reasons.

- Most people find single-spaced writing a bit difficult to read.
- The person assessing your work may wish to add comments or corrections directly onto the text, either on paper, or using VLE tools such as Feedback Studio (Blackboard) and this is not possible when the line spacing is too narrow.

Paragraph formatting

Task

Paragraph formatting

Look at the four versions of work below. What differences do you notice in the formatting of paragraphs? Which version is *not* acceptable? Why?

A

Howells (op cit, 1995) discussed the growing significance of age-weighted pupil numbers (AWPU) in making schools compete with each other for 'clients': something which, he argued, the Government encouraged. He asserted: 'These were not major issues for headteachers a generation ago, but we ignore them today at our peril' (p 45).

The culture and climate of education was changing and with the change came a new vocabulary. A key word in the lexicon of the 1988 National Curriculum was *entitlement*. Every child was to be entitled to a broad and balanced curriculum which was similar in every school in the country. However, schools which could attract more pupils would be better off financially and therefore be likely to be able to deliver the curriculum using better resources.

B

Howells (op cit, 1995) discussed the growing significance of age-weighted pupil numbers (AWPU) in making schools compete with each other for 'clients': something which, he argued, the Government encouraged. He asserted: 'These were not major issues for headteachers a generation ago, but we ignore them today at our peril' (p 45).

The culture and climate of education was changing and with the change came a new vocabulary. A key word in the lexicon of the 1988 National Curriculum was *entitlement*. Every child was to be entitled to a broad and balanced curriculum which was similar in every school in the country. However, schools which could attract more pupils would be better off financially and therefore be likely to be able to deliver the curriculum using better resources.

C

Howells (op cit, 1995) discussed the growing significance of age-weighted pupil numbers (AWPU) in making schools compete with each other for 'clients': something which, he argued, the Government encouraged. He asserted: 'These were not major issues for headteachers a generation ago, but we ignore them today at our peril' (p 45).
The culture and climate of education was changing and with the change came a new vocabulary. A key word in the lexicon of the 1988 National Curriculum was *entitlement*. Every child was to be entitled to a broad and balanced curriculum which was similar in every school in the country. However, schools which could attract more pupils would be better off financially and therefore be likely to be able to deliver the curriculum using better resources.

D

Howells (op cit, 1995) discussed the growing significance of age-weighted pupil numbers (AWPU) in making schools compete with each other for 'clients': something which, he argued, the Government encouraged. He asserted: 'These were not major issues for headteachers a generation ago, but we ignore them today at our peril' (p 45).

The culture and climate of education was changing and with the change came a new vocabulary. A key word in the lexicon of the 1988 National Curriculum was *entitlement*. Every child was to be entitled to a broad and balanced curriculum which was similar in every school in the country. However, schools which could attract more pupils would be better off financially and therefore be likely to be able to deliver the curriculum using better resources.

Discussion: paragraph formatting

Most people find A difficult to read because the paragraphs are not clearly distinguished. B, C and D distinguish paragraphs in different ways: B has a line space between paragraphs; C starts each paragraph with an indentation. D uses both a line space and indentation. If there is indentation, the line space is not strictly necessary, but it does serve to make the distinction between paragraphs even clearer. It is very important that paragraphs are clearly distinguished. This ties in with the discussion in Chapter 2, where you saw how 'cohesive' paragraphs deal with a single, unified idea. Your formatting should underline this sense of cohesion.

CROSS
REFERENCE

Chapter 2,
Coherent
texts and
arguments,
Cohesion and
paragraph
structure

Formatting tables and diagrams

It is important that tables and diagrams are labelled clearly and consistently. The examples below show the typical convention in academic writing, ie tables are labelled at the top, and diagrams are labelled at the bottom. If tables and diagrams are taken or adapted from other sources, they should be clearly referenced. The use of **bold** in labels should follow assessment guidelines; if this is not specified, just make sure you are consistent.

Example of a table:

Table 9.4: Schools' Involvement In Collaboration With Other Schools

School	No. on roll	Stage of cluster development (see Huckman, 1998)	Level of cluster development (see Hargreaves, in Bridges and Husbands, 1996)
NEWBY CE	61	1	1
LOXLEY CE	64	1	1
DARRINGTON	70	2*	2*
KIRKBY CE	93	1	not yet at 1
BARRATT GM	96	1	not yet at 1
CHARLTON CE	135	2*	2*
ST KEVIN'S	168	not yet at 1	not yet at 1
GRIMSTON	234	1	1
OAKWELL	284	1	1
BORCHESTER	314	1	1
MILBURN	323	1	1
TURF MOOR	665	2	2

*with some elements of 3

Example of a figure:

%
12
10
8
6
4
2
0
2012   2013   2014   2015   2016
Year

Figure 2: Percentage of schools in England without dedicated sports facilities in these areas (Triggle, 2017)

If you have included tables and figures, make sure that you have referred to them clearly in the text, eg:

- As Table 1 shows/illustrates, …

- As can be seen in Table 1, …

- Figure 2 shows/illustrates …

- The RDA increases according to age (Table 1).

- Waiting times continue to rise (Figure 2).

Presentation

First impressions are important. The way your assignment looks says a lot about your approach to your studies. A well-presented piece of work shows that you are professional, pay attention to detail, and care about your work. It signals respect for the people who have set and will mark the assessment. It is not about decorating your work or making it striking to look at; it is about creating a document which is professional, clear and easy to navigate.

What should my essay look like?

1) It should have a title page

This should be the first sheet. Even if you are required to use a standard cover sheet for your assignments, there is no reason why you cannot also have a title page. You may be provided with guidelines on what to include, but if not, you may wish to include some or all of the following:

- your name (or your Student ID Number if the assignment is to be submitted anonymously, which it nearly always is nowadays);

- the institution for which it is being submitted, eg 'University of Towncaster – School of Education';
- the title of the assignment;
- the course/module/programme for which it was written (including the date you commenced the course);
- the date of submission or the date you completed the assessment;
- your course unit leader's name and/or your academic adviser's name.

An example is given below:

The University of Towncaster
School of Education

BA (Hons)

(2017 Cohort)

EDUC1674 Life Long Learning

Reflective Essay

Student: 0012345

Submission date: 6th October 2017

Course Unit Lead: Dr Colin Lead

Academic Adviser: Dr Ann Adviser

---

2) The word count should be written on the document

Make it very clear that you have met the word limit by writing the word count at the end of the document. In Microsoft Word, the word count of a document is clearly visible in the bottom left-hand corner of the screen.

3) Your pages should be numbered

If you or a lecturer prints out copies, it is very easy to get things in the wrong order if the pages are not secured together. In Microsoft Word, page numbers are added using the 'insert' tool on the toolbar. You can format these in a number of ways (eg bottom of the page, top of the page, centred, right-hand corner, left-hand corner). Experiment until you find a style that suits you, or that works well with a particular document.

4) It should be written using an appropriate font

Academic work should be written in a font which is easy to read and appropriately 'serious'. This may be specified in the guidelines. If not, use either:

- Times New Roman
- Arial

Inappropriate fonts include:

- Comic Sans

Comic Sans is a popular, 'friendly' font, but it tends to make documents look childish (which explains why it is used in many primary schools).

In Microsoft Word, font (and size – see below) can be easily selected from the toolbar.

5) The font size should be readable and appropriate

Don't use too large or too small a font size. A font size of 12pt is ideal; anything above font size 14pt will appear rather childish, and anything below 10pt will be far too small to read comfortably. Larger font sizes may be used for headings and subheadings. Again, this may be specified in the assessment guidelines.

6) It should look professional

Do not decorate your scripts with fancy pictures and colours. Aim for a professional look, rather than a decorative or striking one.

7) It should follow printing guidelines

Many universities now require you to submit your written assessments electronically, but on those occasions when you are required to print out hard copies, check guidelines on whether you should print on both sides or on one side only. You may need to print out hard copies of documents for your **portfolio**.

And finally ...

Finding advice and support

Universities provide a range of academic writing support. This goes by different names, including 'insessional classes', 'academic literacy support' and 'study skills', and will cover academic writing and other skills, such as speaking or critical thinking. The provision may distinguish between home students and international students, or it may be aimed at both sets of students. This type of integrated provision is becoming more common as it has been recognised that the most problematic issues in academic writing, such as coherence and style, affect all students, not just international students. Of course, students who speak English as a second language may also need specific English-language support, and many universities offer classes in areas such as grammar and pronunciation.

As well as academic writing classes, most universities have 'writing consultations', sometimes known as 'writing tutorials'. These involve meeting with an expert in English language and academic skills to discuss a piece of your writing. The length of these consultations varies, but they usually range from 30 minutes to an hour. You are usually required to send the work in advance. This could be an assignment for which you have already received a mark and feedback, or an assignment which you are currently working on. In the former case, the tutor will be able to help you understand why you received the mark and the feedback you did. In the latter case, the tutor will be able to give you advice on how to improve the piece of work before submission. In both cases, the real focus is not on that particular piece of work, but on you as a developing academic writer: it is a formative consultation rather than a proofreading service. The tutor may help you to correct some errors of grammar, punctuation and style, but they are more likely to focus on issues of clarity, coherence, style and readability. The advice you receive should help you develop your academic writing skills and apply these to future work. The fact that the tutor may not be an expert in the aspect of education you are writing about is actually an advantage, as it will provide a test of whether your explanations of concepts and theories are accessible to a non-expert, as they should be. If you do want help with a piece of work in progress, make sure you leave enough time before submission, as it can take a few weeks to go through the university's booking system.

Summary

This chapter has guided you through the process of preparing your work for submission so as to meet the expectations of your lecturers at university. It has advised you on how to approach the final editing and proofreading process, and it has discussed the issues surrounding proofreading. It has provided you with information and guidance on formatting and presentation, and a presentation 'checklist' that you can apply to any piece of work before submitting it. Finally, it has offered advice on what you can do if you feel you need further professional support with your writing. You should now be ready to submit your writing for assessment, confident in the knowledge that you have done all you can to meet the expectations of your lecturers.

Sources of example texts

Jolliffe, W and Waugh, D with Carss, A (2015) *Teaching Systematic Synthetic Phonics in Primary Schools*. 2nd ed. London: Sage.

Waugh, D (2015) England: Primary Schooling. In Brock, C (ed) *Education in the United Kingdom*. London: Bloomsbury.

Waugh, D, Warner, C and Waugh, R (2016) *Teaching Grammar, Punctuation and Spelling in Primary Schools*. 2nd ed. London: Sage.

Appendix 1
English language references

This is not meant to be an exhaustive list of resources, but rather a selection of those that we think you may find most useful.

Dictionaries

There are many online dictionaries, but if you prefer to feel the weight of one in your hands, then Chambers is a good choice:

Chambers 21st Century Dictionary (1999) Edinburgh: Chambers Harrap Publishers Ltd.

A good online dictionary, especially for students whose first language is not English, is the Cambridge Dictionary. The definitions are very clear and easy to understand, and there is an excellent pronunciation tool:

Cambridge Dictionary. [online] Available at: http://dictionary.cambridge.org/ (accessed 26 March 2017).

Grammar books

Caplan, N (2012) *Grammar Choices for Graduate and Professional Writers*. Ann Arbor, MI: University of Michigan Press.

Caplan's book is aimed at postgraduate students (known as 'graduate' students in the USA, where this book is published). Nevertheless, if you are looking for a systematic analysis of English grammar in the context of academic English, you may find this book very useful. It contains many clear examples of grammar in use in real-life academic writing.

Hewings, M (2015) *Advanced Grammar in Use*. 3rd ed. Cambridge: Cambridge University Press.

Murphy, R (2015) *English Grammar in Use*. 4th ed. Cambridge: Cambridge University Press.

Murphy, R (2015) *Essential Grammar in Use*. 4th ed. Cambridge: Cambridge University Press.

The Grammar in Use series is particularly useful for students whose first language is not English. The books present each grammar point in a clear and systematic way, and provide exercises and a self-study answer key. There are also lots of multimedia features in recent editions.

Other resources

Academic Phrasebank. [online] Available at: www.phrasebank.manchester.ac.uk/ (accessed 14 May 2017).

Academic Word List. Available at: www.victoria.ac.nz/lals/resources/ academicwordlist (accessed 2 April 2017).

Baily, S (2011) *Academic Writing for International Students of English*. 3rd ed. Oxon: Routledge.

Bottomley, J (2014) *Academic Writing for International Students of Science*. Oxon: Routledge.

Peck, J and Cole, M (2012) *Write it Right: The Secrets of Effective Writing*. 2nd ed. New York: Palgrave Macmillan.

Swales, J and Feak, C (2012) *Academic Writing for Graduate Students: Essential Tasks and Skills*. 3rd ed. Michigan: Michigan ELT.

Appendix 2
Grammatical terminology

GRAMMATICAL TERM	DEFINITION	EXAMPLES
adjective	a word which describes a **noun**	a <u>young</u> child a <u>diagnostic</u> test
adverb	a word which adds information to a **verb** or an **adjective**	read <u>daily</u> a <u>very</u> difficult test
article	the words 'a/an' and 'the', used with **nouns**	<u>a</u> classroom <u>the</u> phonics programme
clause	a structure containing a **verb**, forming a sentence, or joining with other clauses to form sentences	(1) <u>This essay aims to explore current approaches to early reading.</u> (1) <u>The child could not take the text</u> (2) <u>because of his heading impairment.</u> (1) <u>Introduced in the late 1980s,</u> (2) <u>the National Curriculum has been revised several times.</u>
conjunction (linking word/phrase)	a word or phrase that joins words, phrases or **clauses**	Grammar <u>and</u> punctuation should be taught <u>but</u> only in context. The child could not take the text (main clause) <u>because</u> of his hearing impairment (subordinate clause). <u>If</u> children are to succeed in school (subordinate clause), reading must be taught in a systematic and structured way (main clause).
contraction	two words joined by an apostrophe	<u>She's</u> in Year 4 <u>it's</u> time for assembly
countable noun*	a **noun** which can be counted and so can be used in the **plural**	a <u>loaf, loaves</u> the <u>child, children</u>

GRAMMATICAL TERM	DEFINITION	EXAMPLES
main clause	the **clause** containing the main idea in a **sentence**	This essay aims to explore approaches to early reading. The child could not take the test because of his hearing impairment. Introduced in the late 1980s, the National Curriculum has been revised several times.
noun	people, places or things	child, school, honesty, training
participle clause	a **clause** with an '–ing' or '–ed' verb form adding information to the **main clause**	Introduced in the late 1980s, the National Curriculum has been revised several times. The study investigated teachers' attitudes to children's literature, using a mixed methods approach.
plural	the form of a **noun** that refers to more than one, usually ending in 's' in English	books, teachers, dishes (regular) women, children, criteria (irregular plurals)
possessive	a word or phrase which denotes belonging	her child Mrs Brown's child the child is hers
proper noun	a noun written with a capital letter, as it is the name of a person, place, company etc	Susan, Doncaster, SATs, NLT, Scholastic
sentence	a group of words usually beginning with a capital letter and ending in a full stop, and containing a **subject** and a **verb**; the main building blocks of writing	Students are advised to make an appointment with their academic adviser. Individual research projects also have much to tell us. A prolific contributor to this debate has been Gemma Moss. Moss makes the case that teacher input is 'crucial'.
singular	the form of a **noun** that refers to one of something	a class a teacher

GRAMMATICAL TERM	DEFINITION	EXAMPLES
subject	the person or thing which the **verb** relates to and agrees with in number	<u>Students</u> are advised to make an appointment with their academic adviser. <u>Topping found</u> that 'boys are more interested in non-fiction'.
that-clause	a **subject/verb** structure that follows certain verbs etc that are usually followed by 'that'	Topping found <u>that 'boys are more interested in non-fiction'</u>.
uncountable noun*	a **noun** seen as a mass which cannot be split or counted, and so cannot be **plural**	pleasure, time, energy, flour, life
quantifier	a word or phrase which denotes 'how much' of a **noun**	<u>few</u> people <u>a large amount of</u> money
verb	a word expressing an action or state	be, is, go, write, take, deliver, improve Students <u>are</u> advised to make an appointment with their academic adviser. Topping <u>found</u> that 'boys are more interested in non-fiction'.

*This is often about how a noun is interpreted in a particular context, rather than an absolute concept. Many nouns can be countable or uncountable depending on the context, eg:

He did it three times.

Time is of the essence.

You only get one life.

Life is a gift.

Cats are said to have nine lives.

Appendix 3
Key phrases in assignments

PHRASE	LEVEL	MEANING
analyse	Mostly Levels 5 and 6, especially with the word 'critically'; rarely Level 4	Look at the concepts and ideas under discussion in depth; the addition of 'critically' means look at the concepts and ideas in depth **and** with a critical eye
assess	All levels, though common at lower levels	Make comments about the value/importance of the concepts and ideas under discussion
compare	All levels, though common at lower levels	Look for similarities between the concepts and ideas under discussion
contrast	All levels, though common at lower levels	Look for differences between the concepts and ideas under discussion; often used with 'compare' (see above)
define	All levels, though common at lower levels	State precisely what is meant by a particular issue, theory or concept
discuss	Level 5 and above; sometimes Level 4	Give reasons for and against; investigate and examine by argument
evaluate	Mostly Levels 5 and 6, especially with the word 'critically'	Weigh up the arguments surrounding an issue, using your own opinions and, more importantly, reference to the work of others
illustrate	All levels	Make clear by the use of examples
outline	All levels, though tends to be used with the lower levels	Give the main features of
review	All levels, though 'critically review' would imply Level 5 and above	Extract relevant information from a document or set of documents
state	All levels, though tends to be used with the lower levels	Present in a clear, concise form
summarise	All levels, though tends to be used with the lower levels	Give an account of all the main points of the concepts and ideas under discussion
with reference to	All levels	Use a specific context, issue or concept to make the meaning clear

Appendix 4
Academic levels at university

UNDERGRADUATE STUDY			
England, Wales, Northern Ireland	**Scotland**	**Award**	**Notes**
Level 4	Level 7	Certificate of Higher Education (CertHE)	
Level 5	Level 8	Diploma of Higher Education (DipHE) Foundation Degree (FdD)	
Level 6	Level 9	Ordinary Bachelor Degree eg BA Education	Minimum academic qualification for teachers in England and Wales
	Level 10	Bachelor Degree with Honours eg BA (Hons) Education, BEd (Hons)	Usual academic qualification for teachers and teachers in England, Wales and Northern Ireland
POSTGRADUATE STUDY			
Level 7	Level 11	Masters Degree, eg MSc, MA, MPhil Postgraduate Certificate or Diploma (PGCert; PGDip)	Useful qualification for those wishing to advance their career
Level 8	Level 12	Research Doctorate (PhD) Professional Doctorate	Useful qualification for advancing careers, especially for working on teacher education in universities

Answer key

Chapter 1
Reflective essays, Task (pages 23–24)

A   Description of a situation and feelings

B   Analysis of feelings

C/D Action taken at the time, exploration of the issues, resulting outcomes, understanding achieved, future action identified

Chapter 2
Organisational frameworks, Task (pages 32–35)

1)

A Classification: factors that might influence a child's reading ability

B Classification: 1) how we communicate, 2) who we communicate to

C Problem–solution: ways of developing culture of literacy

D Classification: responses to autism diagnosis – perhaps chronological stages

E Cause–effect (reasons for drop in applications) and problem–solution

F Compares and contrasts alternative viewpoints in the literature

2)

A

Introduction/background – refer to title

- Definition of teacher
- Definition of well-being
- Concept of 'empowerment'
- Factors influencing a child's well-being (home background, environment, lifestyle, socio-economic status, cultural factors, health, learning difficulties)
- Extent to which teachers can influence
- Compare with influence of other professionals, eg health professionals, social workers, school support staff
- Contextualise to my area of teaching

Conclusion – can have an impact, but other factors (eg home background, environment, lifestyle, socio-economic status, cultural factors, health, learning difficulties) are important too – potential of teachers to influence these things?

B

Introduction/background – claimed that communication is the core skill of teaching

- Definition of communication

- Different forms of communication: pupils, families, colleagues, partner organisations
- Relative importance of (other) different core skills (pedagogic skills, intellectual skills, subject knowledge) – are these less important than communication?
- Problems caused by breakdown in communication
- How communication impacts on other aspects of teaching – thus more important?
- Is communication more of a concern for school managers than classroom teachers?

Conclusion – teachers need a range of skills but communication is integral to all, and very difficult to be a good teacher without good communication skills, even if competent in 'technical' skills.

General and specific information, Task (page 41)

General:

Children need to be able to hear the separate sounds, or phonemes, in words, and to produce them.

Specific: problem

English is a phonologically complex language, with (depending a little on regional accents) 20 vowel phonemes, such as /aw/ and /ai/, and 24 consonant phonemes, such as /f/ and /ch/. The consonant phonemes can be combined in 49 different clusters at the beginning or end of syllables, including clusters of three such as the cluster at the beginning of 'straight'.

Specific: consequence

Children take a long time to learn to produce all the English phonemes accurately in all positions in words.

Specific: some of the problems which arise

Their early speech is full of phonological simplifications such as 'bo' for 'ball', 'guck' for 'duck' and 'bikkit' for 'biscuit'. This can make their speech difficult to understand.

Old and new information, Task (page 42)

Bold refers back to information underlined

Children need to be able to combine words in order to communicate more complex meanings than can be conveyed by single words. They have to learn the rules that govern how words can be combined into sentences; for example, basic word order in English is subject, verb, object (eg The boy ate the apple), but **this** is not the case in all languages. From single words children start to combine two words, often using words such as 'more' and 'no' in combination with many other words. Utterances become longer and longer, particularly once the word 'and' begins to be used, and grammatical complexity also increases, with a wider range of connectives used to express more sophisticated meanings, and increasing ability to express negatives and ask questions.

Noun or pronoun?, Task (pages 43–44)

The National Reading Panel in the USA has summed up (2000) research on vocabulary development by citing nine implications for reading instruction. They suggest that vocabulary should be taught in the classroom both directly and indirectly, and that repetition and multiple exposures to new items are important. Learning in rich contexts is important for learning vocabulary, and tasks based on it should be restructured when this is necessary to make meaning clear. Learning vocabulary should always entail active involvement in learning tasks, including the use of computer technology to help teach it. Vocabulary can also be acquired through incidental learning. Finally the study suggests that it is important to remember that how vocabulary is assessed and evaluated can have different effects on instruction, and that dependence on a single method for teaching it will not result in optimal learning.

Notes

Other combinations are possible; the important thing to remember is to avoid ambiguity and to be sensitive to the reader's need to be reminded of the topic frequently.

Referring back in the text to summarise and comment, Task (pages 46–47)

1)

The writer summarises and signals her attitude by using the following phrases:

a) This is a dense document

b) arcane discussions

c) drawing a vague set of conclusions

d) incorrect or seriously compromised by the true facts

2)

a) case

b) view

c) problem

d) approach

e) approach

f) approach

3)

a) this

b) these

c) such

d) these

Linking ideas, Task (pages 49–50)

1)

a) Data were collected on the activities of 25 students on teaching practice placements in primary schools. In addition, interviews were carried out over a three-week period.

b) A number of students reported that they had been given insufficient support, particularly in response to difficult situations. In contrast, others praised their school-based tutors for the support they had given them.

c) Some students were involved in the communities where their placement schools were situated, albeit in different social contexts.

d) Phonics is one of the systems whereby children learn to read with confidence.

e) Shared writing exercises in the class give pupils a good model, thereby encouraging them to express their own ideas.

f) The report explored the needs of a subgroup of special needs pupils, namely, those with dyslexia and learning difficulties.

g) It was reported that most children said they enjoyed English and Maths lessons (84% and 81% respectively).

h) There are concerns of a 'two-tier' system comprising teachers who have taken a PGCE qualification and those who have undertaken school-based QTS training, with the former having more status, and the latter being seen as a less professional option.

2)

Dyslexia is a common learning difficulty that can cause problems with reading, writing and spelling. ~~Furthermore~~, it is a 'specific learning difficulty', which means it causes problems with certain abilities used for learning, such as reading and writing. ~~However~~, it has been estimated that up to one in every ten to twenty people in the UK has some degree of dyslexia. Given that dyslexia is a lifelong problem that can present challenges on a daily basis, but support is available to improve reading and writing skills and help those with the problem be successful at school and work. ~~While~~ signs of dyslexia usually become apparent when a child starts school and begins to focus more on learning how to read and write. However, people with dyslexia often have good skills in other areas, such as creative thinking and problem solving.

Chapter 3

Referencing errors, Task (pages 66–67)

1)

a) There is no publication year, which name–year (Harvard) systems require:

> According to Jolliffe and Waugh (2012), four modes of language interrelate to produce literacy.

b) This citation is information-prominent. Both the name and the date should be in brackets, and at the end of the sentence and before the full stop:

> The major hindrance appears to be the cultural dominance of 'technical rationality' (Schön, 1988).

c) Alphabetical sequencing is required to distinguish between two publications in the same year:

> In a theoretical paper, Dickoff and James (1968a) argue this position, which is subsequently backed up by a further, data-based paper (Dickoff and James, 1968b).

d) Round, rather than square, brackets are the norm:

> Meleis (2001) speculates that historical and cultural paternalism are largely to blame.

e) This citation is a direct quotation so the quotation must be enclosed in speech marks and the page number must be provided. Since it's a quotation that actively involves the author's name, the year needs to be in brackets:

> To quote from Johnston and Watson (2007, p 26): 'Learners acquire phoneme awareness better in the context of letters and print compared to learning without this concrete support.'

Alternatively:

> To quote from Johnston and Watson (2007): 'Learners acquire phoneme awareness better in the context of letters and print compared to learning without this concrete support' (p 26).

f) The authors' initials are not required in the main body of text* (only the final reference list):

> According to Gill and Waugh (2017), teachers use many activities to attune learners to sounds all around them.

*There is an exception when you have authors with the same surname who have published in the same year and you want to distinguish between them in your work. For example, if you had used a book by Mary Green from 2008 and also one by Helen Green from 2008, you'd refer to the first as M Green (2008) and the second as H Green (2008).

g) With two or more authors, you use 'et al' in the main body of text (but list all authors in the final reference list):

> The results are consistent with the findings of Posner et al (2012).

h) Round brackets are required rather than square ones, and there is no year for Smith:

> Smith (1989, cited by Jones 1992) suggests that the findings are incomplete.

i) The following is more academic:

> ... (see, for example, the 'change spiral' of Lewin, 1958).

j) The citation actively involves the author (is author-prominent) so the brackets need to go round the year only:

> Schön (1988) suggests that this paradox can be resolved by acknowledging the importance of subjectivity.

2)

Note that there may be slight variations in styles across publishers and departments.

a) Crystal, D (2005) *How Language Works*. London: Penguin.

b) DCSF (2008) *Teaching Effective Vocabulary: What Can Teachers Do to Increase the Vocabulary of Children Who Start Education with a Limited Vocabulary?* Nottingham: DCSF.

c) DfE (2013) *The National Curriculum in England: Key Stages 1 and 2 Framework Document*. London: DfE.

d) Dombey, H (2009) *ITE English: Readings for discussion December 2009*. [online] Available at: www.ite.org.uk/ite_readings/simple_view_reading.pdf (accessed 18 March 2018).

e) Ings, R (2009) *Writing Is Primary: Action Research on the Teaching of Writing in Primary Schools*. Esmée Fairburn Foundation. [online] Available at: www.nawe.co.uk/Private/17646/Live/Writing-is-Primary.pdf (accessed 18 March 2018).

f) Meek, M (2010) Readings about Reading. *Changing English: Studies in Culture and Education*, 11(2), 307–17.

g) National Reading Panel (2000) *Teaching Children to Read: An Evidence-Based Assessment of the Scientific Research Literature on Reading and Its Implications for Reading Instruction. Reports of Subgroups*. NICHD. [online] Available at: www.dysadd.com/resources/SpecialEd/TeachingChildrenToRead.pdf (accessed 2 April 2018).

h) Rooke, J (2013) *Transforming Writing: Evaluation Report*. London: Literacy Trust. [online] Available at: www.literacytrust.org.uk/assets/0001/9256/Transforming_Writing_Final_Report.pdf (accessed 17 January 2018).

Focus, Task (pages 71–73)

1)

Information-prominent: b, d, f
Author-prominent: a, c, e

2)

a) <u>As</u> Wright (1993) <u>points out</u>, one of the paradoxes of successful change is that it escapes public notice simply because it is successful.

c) <u>According to</u> Oster (2011), cooperative learning has been used to develop a wide range of purposeful learning for primary-aged pupils.

e) Warrington et al (2013) <u>argue that</u> teaching will only really develop as a profession if teachers become more political.

3)

a) advocate

b) identify/identified

c) acknowledge

d) distinguishes between

e) argues that

f) acknowledges that or argues that

Chapter 4

Being concise, Task (pages 77–78)

Square brackets, eg [the country of] = unnecessary or less concise

Strike through, eg ~~whole wide~~ = delete as completely redundant or tautological

Words in round brackets, eg (in) = suggested more concise alternatives

Roald Dahl was born in [the country of] Wales, but his parents came from [the country of] Norway. Roald Dahl was [a member of] (in) the Royal Air Force in the Second World War, [which took place between the years of] (between) 1939 and 1945. In the 1940s, Roald Dahl [began to become] (became) well-known for writing stories for both children and adults, and [he] eventually became one of the best-selling writers of stories in the ~~whole wide~~ world. [Roald] Dahl's [books for children] (children's books) are often very ~~comical and funny and~~ humorous, as well as [being] quite scary and frightening. [Roald] Dahl's [books for children] (children's books) are ~~many and~~ numerous and [they] include [books such as] *The Witches, The Magic Finger, Fantastic Mr Fox, James and the Giant Peach, Charlie and the Chocolate Factory, Matilda, The BFG, The Twits,* ~~as well as others like~~ (and) *George's Marvellous Medicine.* His stories for adults ~~and grown-ups~~ include ~~books like~~ *Tales of the Unexpected* and Kiss Kiss.

Being precise, Task (page 78)

1) evolved
2) commitment
3) determine
4) exhibiting
5) administer
6) diagnostic
7) in terms of
8) associated with

Identifying inappropriate language, Task (page 82)

1) male/man/~~bloke~~
2) inebriated/~~tipsy~~/drunk
3) ~~impecunious~~/poor/~~broke~~
4) food/nutrition/~~grub~~
5) sleep/~~slumber~~/~~doze~~

Identifying formal language, Task (page 83)

1) Little
2) deteriorated
3) was awarded
4) approximately
5) adhere; enshrined within
6) demonstrate
7) ensure
8) such as
9) improve
10) facilitate
11) An increasing number of
12) many

Improving style, Task (page 84)

A suggested alternative:

The strong economy means that fewer people seek teaching careers and many schools are finding recruitment challenging. Governmental support is often limited and many face cuts in funding.

Lack of Government funding may inhibit their ability to deliver high-quality education. Many outstanding teachers become disillusioned by the perceived criticism from politicians and the media.

Without increased funding to improve salaries, recruitment may become increasingly challenging.

Commonly confused words, Task (pages 87–88)

1) practice
2) practise
3) advice
4) advise
5) device
6) devised

7) licensed
8) licence
9) effects
10) affected
11) their
12) There

Variation in comma use, Task (pages 91–92)

B separates phrases and clauses using commas; A does not always do this and sentences are quite long. It is arguably easier for the reader to have more commas to make the distinction between clauses clearer.

Grammar and punctuation, Task (pages 94–95)

Making statements into questions

Word order, mentioned earlier, can also be important in English when we want to make a statement into a question. Sometimes we do not need to change the order at all. For example:

You want some tea.

You want some tea?

Here, the change from a full stop to a question mark at the end of the sentence changes the way we say the sentence and what it means.

In spoken language, we have, in recent years, become used to the so-called 'interrogative intonation', often through exposure to Australian soaps such as *Neighbours* and *Home and Away*. This means the way in which the voice rising at the end of a sentence can often make a simple declarative sentence sound like a question: 'I come from Sydney?' Interestingly, this pattern of rising tone is similar in many languages, including French, German, Spanish and dialects of Mandarin Chinese.

Media literacy

An Ofcom survey of children's media use in 2014 showed that in the UK children's use of a variety of devices to go online is increasing at home (Ofcom, 2014). That use could be for a variety of purposes and whilst the report does not look specifically at children writing digitally, it does provide an insight into activities which almost certainly include digital writing. Clearly text messaging is a significant part of that and it is probably safe to assume that the 32% of 8 to 11-year-olds who own a phone will use text messages and the 20% who own smartphones may also use those for email or other text creation.

(Adapted from Bennett, J (2015) Beyond Pen and Paper. In Waugh, D, Neaum, S and Bushnell, A (eds) *Beyond Early Writing*. Northwich: Critical Publishing)

Parallel structures, Task (pages 96–97)

Possible responses:

1) When diagnosing reading problems, teachers need to be aware of the impact on pupils, classes and the school as a whole.

2) One initiative for working with parents to provide help, guidance and support aimed to:

- improve pupil outcomes;
- promote child development;
- involve fathers as well as mothers;
- support for looked-after children.

3) Pupils with English as an additional language (EAL) may find social engagement challenging. Teachers need to be aware that in some cases previous traumatic experiences may continue to affect children. They will also need to explore extent of prior school attendance in pupils' country of origin, as well as finding out about parental understanding of English.

Chapter 5
Proofreading practice, Task (page 105)

A

It is important when looking at children's work to separate careless mistakes from genuine spelling problems. You may not feel that it is desirable to correct every error in each child's work, but some people would argue that it is not only important but necessary if each child is to fulfil their potential. A few minutes spent helping children to acquire a familiarity with common spellings wouldn't go amiss in many classrooms. Unfortunately, many teachers do not see the value of teaching spelling and its importance is thus diminished in children's eyes.

B

Teachers may feel it is all right to quickly scan a piece of work looking for mistakes and then tell a child to check their work, but this practice may not help the child to supplement his spelling repertoire.

I believe that children's spelling improves when they perceive spelling as an important aspect of writing, but are not afraid to experiment with words and don't show any reluctance to make use of a dictionary.

NB

In academic writing, it is not usually acceptable to use contractions such as *wouldn't*.

It can sometimes be tricky to know what is and isn't acceptable in formal English, as there is no single national body (like the Academie Française in France) making decisions on this. Individuals and even dictionaries disagree on certain language choices. *Alright*, although increasingly accepted, is defined in some dictionaries as a common misspelling of *all right*. If at all unsure, choose the most formal option.

Personally speaking, I am of the opinion is unnecessary. If the first person is permitted, it would be better simply to state: *I believe* …

Media literacy

An Ofcom survey of children's media use in 2014 showed that in the UK children's use of a variety of devices to go online is increasing at home (Ofcom, 2014). That use could be for a variety of purposes and whilst the report does not look specifically at children writing digitally, it does provide an insight into activities which almost certainly include digital writing. Clearly, text messaging is a significant part of that and it is probably safe to assume that the 32% of 8-11-year-olds who own a phone will use text messages, and the 20% who own smartphones may also use those for email or other text creation.

Index

Note: *italicised* page numbers are illustrations, **bold** page numbers are tables, and the suffix 'a' refers to the Appendix at the back of the book.